WHAT'S FOR DINNER

WHAT'S FOR DINNER

A COOKBOOK OF
100+ SOLUTIONS
TO THE ULTIMATE QUESTION

CIDER MILL
PRESS

BOOK
PUBLISHERS
KENNEBUNKPORT, MAINE

CONTENTS

INTRODUCTION

What's for dinner?

For many, that has come to be the most pressing, consistently baffling, and stressful question they face on a day-to-day basis.

Its status as a trial is due to its generality. It is a question that leads to an endless amount of other questions: Do I try my hand at something new? Turn to an old standard? Go vegetarian after last night's heavy, savory dish? What do I have energy for? What's at home in the pantry that I can make use of? What does everyone else in the house want?

Worst of all, this deluge typically comes at the end of the day, when energy and patience are at their nadir, and the thought of formulating a plan, running to the store and battling the crowds there, prepping a meal at home, and cleaning up afterward become almost unbearable. The demands of modern life being what they are, most people just throw up their hands and default to takeout, leftovers, or something tucked away in the freezer.

Blessedly, those days are past.

Now you can confidently turn toward the evening knowing that a tasty, nutritious, and unique preparation awaits. Not only that, you can be sure that this dish will fit nicely into whatever amount of time, energy, and attention you happen to have.

No matter what dark alley the dinner question leads you down, we've armed you with an answer. Company popping by unexpectedly? There's a series of inventive dishes that will look and taste as though they required far more heavy lifting than they do in reality. One of your children having a rough go and in need of a bit of comfort cooking? There's a whole chapter of easy-to-prepare meals capable of providing solace. Have a bit more time to spend in the kitchen and feel like whipping up something special? The book concludes with a number of dishes that will transform any evening into a special occasion.

The structure of the modern world has made a willingness to plan essential to attaining some peace of mind. This book makes it easier than ever to do that, providing a number of strategies that can cut through the noise and chaos, and allow you to focus on the things you should when the time comes to put something on the table for yourself and those you love.

TIME IS
OF THE
ESSENCE

As the fast-paced and unpredictable world means that a day can assume any one of a thousand shapes, at a moment's notice, one needs a series of stratagems in order to guarantee that a wholesome and satisfying meal ends up on the dinner table. Sometimes that means tucking a protein in a slow cooker or marinade, where it can develop flavor without requiring much hands-on attention. Sometimes that means letting the considerable heat made available by the oven do the work. And sometimes that means tossing whatever's on hand—parts of the previous night's meal, the odds and ends of the pantry—together in a way that seems inspired.

We know how easily dinner can become daunting. We're starting with these meals because we know that if you have a reliable response, managing whatever the world throws at you becomes that much easier.

YIELD: 4 SERVINGS

ACTIVE TIME: 10 MINUTES

TOTAL TIME: 1 HOUR AND 20 MINUTES

GARLIC & BASIL BAKED COD

2 lbs. cod fillets

Salt and pepper, to taste

2 tablespoons finely chopped fresh oregano

1 teaspoon coriander

1 teaspoon paprika

10 garlic cloves, minced

15 basil leaves, shredded

6 tablespoons olive oil

2 tablespoons fresh lemon juice

2 shallots, sliced

2 tomatoes, sliced

1   Place the cod in a mixing bowl or a large resealable plastic bag and add the remaining ingredients, except for the shallots and tomatoes. Stir to combine, place the mixture in the refrigerator, and let the cod marinate for 1 hour, stirring or shaking occasionally.

2   Preheat the oven to 425°F, remove the cod from the refrigerator, and let it come to room temperature. Cover the bottom of a baking dish with the shallots, place the cod on top, and top with the tomatoes. Pour the marinade over the mixture, place it in the oven, and bake for about 15 minutes, until the fish is flaky. Remove from the oven and let the cod rest briefly before serving.

YIELD: 4 SERVINGS

ACTIVE TIME: 15 MINUTES

TOTAL TIME: 25 MINUTES

THAI MUSSELS

2 lbs. mussels, debearded

½ cup packed fresh cilantro

1 tablespoon olive oil

4 shallots, minced

2 garlic cloves, sliced

1 lemongrass stalk, trimmed and cut into 4 large pieces

1 bird's eye chili pepper, stemmed, seeds and ribs removed, and sliced

1 (14 oz.) can of coconut milk

1 tablespoon fish sauce

Juice of 1 lime

½ lb. cooked rice noodles, for serving (optional)

2 cups cooked white rice, for serving (optional)

1   Wash the mussels thoroughly and discard any that aren't tightly closed. Remove the cilantro leaves from the stems. Set the leaves aside and finely chop the stems.

2   Place the olive oil in a Dutch oven and warm it over medium-high heat. When the oil starts to shimmer, add the shallots, garlic, chopped cilantro stems, lemongrass, and the chili and sauté until the garlic starts to brown, about 2 minutes. Stir in the coconut milk and the fish sauce and bring to a boil.

3   Add the mussels and immediately cover the pot. Steam the mussels until the majority of them have opened and the meat is still plump, about 5 minutes. Be careful not to overcook the mussels, as it will cause them to have a rubbery texture. Discard any mussels that do not open.

4   Stir a few times to coat the mussels and add half of the lime juice. Taste and add more lime juice as needed. Garnish with the reserved cilantro leaves and serve over rice noodles or rice.

YIELD: 6 SERVINGS

ACTIVE TIME: 30 MINUTES

TOTAL TIME: 30 MINUTES

CHILI, SHRIMP & BASIL SALAD

FOR THE DRESSING

2 red bird's eye chili peppers

½ cup soy sauce

½ cup sambal oelek

Juice from 3 limes

¼ cup brown sugar

1 tablespoon minced ginger

2 tablespoons curry powder

FOR THE SALAD

½ head of napa cabbage, chopped

1 cup mint leaves, chopped

2 cups basil leaves, chopped

1 cup fresh cilantro, chopped

1 red onion, sliced thin

3 scallions, trimmed and sliced thin

1 carrot, peeled and sliced thin on a bias

1 lb. shrimp, cooked and chopped

¼ cup raw cashews, chopped, for garnish

1 To prepare the dressing, place all of the ingredients in a food processor and blitz until smooth. Set aside.

2 To make the salad, place all of the ingredients, except for the cashews, in a mixing bowl and stir to combine. Add the dressing, toss to coat, top with crushed cashews, and serve.

TIP: This dressing also makes for a wonderful marinade for shrimp and any whitefish, such as halibut or cod.

YIELD: 4 SERVINGS

ACTIVE TIME: 15 MINUTES

TOTAL TIME: 4 HOURS AND 15 MINUTES

SOFRITO & QUINOA SALAD

2 poblano peppers, stemmed and seeded

1 red bell pepper, stemmed and seeded

1 green bell pepper, stemmed and seeded

1 white onion, peeled and cut into quarters

3 plum tomatoes

2 garlic cloves, peeled

1 tablespoon cumin

2 tablespoons adobo seasoning

1½ cups quinoa, rinsed

Toasted pumpkin seeds, for garnish

1 Dice one of the poblanos, half of the bell peppers, and half of the onion. Place the diced vegetables to the side. Place the remaining ingredients, except for the quinoa and the pumpkin seeds, in a food processor and blitz until smooth.

2 Place the diced vegetables, the puree, and the quinoa in a slow cooker and cook on low until the quinoa is tender, about 4 hours.

3 Fluff the quinoa with a fork, garnish with the pumpkin seeds, and serve.

TIP: Sofrito is key to a number of wonderful preparations in Caribbean cuisine, and is capable of lending considerable brightness to a standard baked chicken or fish dish.

YIELD: 4 SERVINGS

ACTIVE TIME: 20 MINUTES

TOTAL TIME: 30 MINUTES

GREEN SHAKSHUKA

1 tablespoon olive oil

1 onion, chopped

2 garlic cloves, minced

½ lb. tomatillos, husked, rinsed, and chopped

1 (12 oz.) package of frozen chopped spinach

1 teaspoon coriander

¼ cup water

Salt and pepper, to taste

8 eggs

Tabasco, to taste

1   Place the olive oil in a large skillet and warm it over medium-high heat. When the oil starts to shimmer, add the onion and sauté until it just starts to soften, about 5 minutes. Add the garlic and cook until fragrant, about 2 minutes. Add the tomatillos and cook until they start to collapse, about 5 minutes.

2   Add the spinach, coriander, and water and cook, breaking up the spinach with a fork, until the spinach is completely defrosted and blended with the tomatillos. Season with salt and pepper.

3   Evenly spread the mixture in the pan and then make eight indentations in it. Crack an egg into each indentation. Reduce the heat to medium, cover the pan, and let the eggs cook until the whites are set, 3 to 5 minutes. Generously sprinkle Tabasco over the top before serving.

YIELD: 4 SERVINGS

ACTIVE TIME: 10 MINUTES

TOTAL TIME: 15 MINUTES

VEAL SCALLOPINI

½ cup all-purpose flour

½ teaspoon grated fresh nutmeg

Salt and pepper, to taste

2 tablespoons unsalted butter

1 lb. veal cutlets, pounded thin

½ cup Beef Stock (see page 205)

¼ cup pitted and sliced green olives

Zest and juice of 1 lemon

1 Warm a large cast-iron skillet over medium heat for 5 minutes.

2 Place the flour, nutmeg, salt, and pepper on a large plate and stir to combine.

3 Place the butter in the pan. When it starts to sizzle, dredge the veal in the seasoned flour until it is coated lightly on both sides. Working in batches, place the veal in the skillet and cook for about 1 minute on each side, until browned and the juices run clear. Set the cooked veal aside.

4 Deglaze the pan with the stock. Add the olives, lemon zest, and lemon juice, stir to combine, and cook until heated through. To serve, plate the veal and pour the pan sauce over each cutlet.

NOTE: If you are not a fan of veal, or are simply looking to switch things up, this same preparation will work just as well with chicken cutlets.

VEGETABLE STOCK

Place 2 tablespoons olive oil, 2 trimmed and well rinsed leeks, 2 peeled and sliced carrots, 2 celery stalks, 2 sliced onions, and 3 unpeeled, smashed garlic cloves in a large stockpot and cook over low heat until the liquid the vegetables release has evaporated. Add 2 sprigs of fresh parsley and thyme, 1 bay leaf, 8 cups water, ½ teaspoon black peppercorns, and salt to taste. Raise the heat to high and bring the stock to a boil. Reduce heat so that the stock simmers and cook for 2 hours, skimming to remove any impurities that float to the surface. Strain the stock through a fine sieve, let the stock cool slightly, and place it in the refrigerator, uncovered, to chill. Remove the fat layer and cover. The stock will keep in the refrigerator for 3 to 5 days, and in the freezer for up to 3 months.

YIELD: 4 SERVINGS

ACTIVE TIME: 15 MINUTES

TOTAL TIME: 30 MINUTES

CRAB & OKRA SOUP

1 cup peanuts, chopped

10 okra pods, sliced into ½-inch rounds

½ cup coconut oil

1 red bell pepper, stemmed, seeds and ribs removed, and diced

1 yellow onion, sliced into half-moons

1 habanero pepper, stemmed, seeds and ribs removed, and chopped

1 large potato, peeled and diced

4 cups Vegetable Stock (see sidebar)

1 cup clam juice

1 cup coconut milk

Salt, to taste

4 cups fresh spinach leaves

1 lb. lump crabmeat

Lime wedges, for serving

1   Place the peanuts in a dry Dutch oven and toast over medium heat until they are browned. Remove them from the pot and set aside. Add the okra and cook, while stirring, until browned all over, about 5 minutes. Remove and set aside.

2   Place the coconut oil in the Dutch oven and warm over medium heat. When it starts to shimmer, add the bell pepper, onion, habanero pepper, and potato and sauté until the onion starts to soften, about 5 minutes.

3   Add the stock and clam juice, bring to a simmer, and cook for 5 minutes. Add the coconut milk, return to a simmer, and season with salt.

4   Working in batches, transfer the soup to a blender and puree until smooth. Return the soup to the Dutch oven and simmer for another 5 minutes. Stir in the peanuts, okra, spinach, and crabmeat and cook until the spinach has wilted, about 4 minutes. Ladle the soup into warmed bowls and serve with lime wedges.

YIELD: 4 SERVINGS   **ACTIVE TIME:** 20 MINUTES   **TOTAL TIME:** 20 MINUTES

VEGGIE BURGERS

1 (14 oz.) can of black beans, drained and rinsed

⅓ cup minced scallions

¼ cup chopped roasted red peppers

¼ cup corn kernels

½ cup panko

1 egg, lightly beaten

2 tablespoons finely chopped fresh cilantro

½ teaspoon cumin

½ teaspoon cayenne pepper

½ teaspoon black pepper

1 teaspoon fresh lime juice

1 tablespoon olive oil

Hamburger buns, for serving

Guacamole (see sidebar), for serving

1   Place half of the beans, the scallions, and roasted red peppers in a food processor and pulse until the mixture is a thick paste. Transfer it to a large bowl.

2   Add the corn, panko, egg, cilantro, cumin, cayenne, black pepper, and lime juice to the bowl and stir to combine. Add the remaining beans and stir vigorously until the mixture holds together.

3   Place a 12-inch cast-iron skillet over medium-high heat and coat the bottom with the olive oil. Form the mixture into four patties. When the oil starts to shimmer, add the patties, cover the skillet, and cook until browned and cooked through, about 5 minutes per side. Serve immediately on hamburger buns with the Guacamole.

TIP: Should you be looking to avoid carbs or trying to use up some greens you have on hand, these veggie burgers are also wonderful served over arugula or mesclun greens.

GUACAMOLE

Place the flesh of 3 avocados in a mixing bowl and mash. Stir in the juice of 2 limes, 2 seeded and chopped tomatoes, 1 chopped red onion, 2 minced garlic cloves, season with salt and pepper, and work the mixture until it is the desired texture. Garnish with finely chopped fresh cilantro and serve.

YIELD: 4 SERVINGS

ACTIVE TIME: 15 MINUTES

TOTAL TIME: 25 MINUTES

DRY-FRIED BEANS

1 tablespoon olive oil, plus more as needed

1 lb. green beans, trimmed

½ lb. ground pork

2 tablespoons Chinese pickled vegetables, chopped

2 garlic cloves, chopped

2 tablespoons sherry

2 tablespoons soy sauce

1 tablespoon fermented black bean garlic sauce

1 teaspoon sugar

2 cups cooked white rice, for serving

1 Place the oil in a large skillet and warm it over high heat. When the oil starts to shimmer, add the beans and let them cook until they start to char, about 5 minutes. Turn the beans over and cook on the other side until they are charred all over. Transfer the beans to a bowl and set aside.

2 Add the pork to the pan and cook it over medium-high heat, breaking it up with a fork as it browns, for about 6 minutes. Add the pickled vegetables and the garlic. Cook, stirring continuously, until the contents of the pan are fragrant. Add more oil if the pan starts to look dry.

3 Add the sherry and cook until it is nearly evaporated. Stir in the soy sauce, fermented black bean garlic sauce, and sugar, return the green beans to the pan, and cook until heated through. Serve over the white rice.

NOTE: Depending on where you live, Chinese pickled vegetables may prove tough to come by, in which case either kimchi or sauerkraut can be comfortably substituted.

YIELD: 4 SERVINGS

ACTIVE TIME: 15 MINUTES

TOTAL TIME: 30 MINUTES

SAAG ALOO

1 tablespoon olive oil

½ lb. fingerling or red potatoes, chopped

1 onion, chopped

1 teaspoon mustard seeds

1 teaspoon cumin

1 garlic clove, chopped

1-inch piece of fresh ginger, peeled and minced

1 lb. frozen chopped spinach

1 teaspoon red pepper flakes

½ cup water

Salt, to taste

2 tablespoons plain yogurt, or to taste

1   Place the olive oil in a large skillet and warm over medium heat. When the oil starts to shimmer, add the potatoes and cook until they start to brown, about 5 minutes.

2   Add the onion, mustard seeds, and cumin and sauté until the onion starts to soften, about 5 minutes. Add the garlic and ginger and cook, stirring constantly, until the mixture is fragrant, about 2 minutes.

3   Stir in the frozen spinach, the red pepper flakes, and water and cover the pan with a lid. Cook, stirring occasionally, until the spinach is heated through, about 10 minutes.

4   Remove the cover and cook until all of the liquid has evaporated. Season with salt, stir in the yogurt, and serve. Add more yogurt if you prefer a creamier dish.

YIELD: 4 SERVINGS

ACTIVE TIME: 15 MINUTES

TOTAL TIME: 30 MINUTES

SUKIYAKI

Salt, to taste

1½ lbs. udon noodles

1 tablespoon olive oil

2 lbs. rib eye, sliced very thin

3 tablespoons brown sugar

½ cup mirin

½ cup sake

¼ cup soy sauce

1 cup water

6 scallions, trimmed and sliced into 2-inch pieces

2 cups chopped napa cabbage

1 bunch of enoki mushrooms

6 large shiitake mushrooms

1 cup fresh spinach

½ lb. tofu, drained and diced

1 Bring water to a boil in a Dutch oven. Add salt and the noodles and cook until the noodles are al dente, about 2 minutes. Drain, rinse with cold water, and set the noodles aside.

2 Place the oil in the Dutch oven and warm it over medium-high heat. When the oil starts to shimmer, add the steak and brown sugar and cook, stirring occasionally, until the steak is browned all over, about 2 minutes. Stir in the mirin, sake, soy sauce, and water.

3 Carefully arrange the noodles, scallions, cabbage, mushrooms, spinach, and tofu in the broth. Cover the pot and steam until the cabbage is wilted, about 5 minutes. Ladle into warmed bowls and serve immediately.

YIELD: 4 SERVINGS

ACTIVE TIME: 20 MINUTES

TOTAL TIME: 20 MINUTES

RED SNAPPER WITH TOMATILLO SAUCE

1 lb. tomatillos, husked, rinsed, and quartered

½ white onion, chopped

1 serrano pepper, stemmed

1 garlic clove, crushed

1 bunch of fresh cilantro, some leaves reserved for garnish

2 tablespoons olive oil

1½ lbs. skinless red snapper fillets

Radish, sliced, for garnish

Guacamole (see page 25), for serving

Corn Tortillas (see page 77), for serving

Lime wedges, for serving

1 Place a dry large cast-iron skillet over high heat and add the tomatillos, onion, and serrano pepper. Cook until the tomatillos and pepper are starting to char, about 5 minutes, and then transfer the vegetables to a food processor. Add the garlic and cilantro and blitz until smooth.

2 Place the oil in the skillet and warm it over medium-high heat. When the oil starts to shimmer, add the red snapper fillets in a single layer and cook until they brown lightly, about 3 to 4 minutes. Do not turn them over.

3 Remove the pan from heat and allow it to cool for a few minutes. Carefully pour the tomatillo sauce over the fish. It will immediately start to simmer. Place the skillet over medium heat and let it simmer until the fish is cooked through, about 4 minutes. Garnish with the reserved cilantro and sliced radish and serve with the Guacamole, tortillas, and lime wedges.

YIELD: 4 SERVINGS

ACTIVE TIME: 5 MINUTES

TOTAL TIME: 10 MINUTES

GARLIC SHRIMP

4 tablespoons unsalted butter, at room temperature

1 lb. shrimp, peeled and deveined

8 garlic cloves, minced

½ teaspoon lemon-pepper seasoning

1 tablespoon fresh lemon juice

1 tablespoon finely chopped fresh chives or parsley, for garnish

1   Place a large cast-iron skillet over medium heat and add the butter. When the butter has melted and is foaming, add the shrimp and cook, without stirring, for 3 minutes. Remove the shrimp from the pan with a slotted spoon and set them aside.

2   Reduce the heat to medium-low and add the garlic and lemon-pepper seasoning. Cook until the garlic has softened, about 2 minutes. Return the shrimp to the pan and cook until warmed through, about 1 minute. To serve, sprinkle the lemon juice over the dish and garnish with the chives or parsley.

YIELD: 6 SERVINGS

ACTIVE TIME: 10 MINUTES

TOTAL TIME: 5 HOURS

SHREDDED CHICKEN WITH BEANS & RICE

2 lbs. boneless, skinless chicken breasts

1 cup Chicken Stock (see sidebar)

1 jalapeño pepper, stemmed, seeds and ribs removed, and minced, plus more for garnish

2 garlic cloves, minced

1½ tablespoons cumin

1 tablespoon garlic powder

1 cup white rice

2 plum tomatoes, chopped

2 tablespoons kosher salt

1 tablespoon black pepper

1 (14 oz.) can of black beans, drained and rinsed

1. Place the chicken, stock, jalapeño, garlic, cumin, and garlic powder in a slow cooker and cook on high until the chicken is very tender and falling apart, about 4 hours. Remove the chicken from the slow cooker, place it in a bowl, and shred it with a fork. Cover the bowl with aluminum foil and set it aside.

2. Add the rice, tomatoes, salt, and black pepper to the slow cooker and cook until the rice is tender, 40 to 50 minutes. Make sure to check on the rice after 30 minutes, since cook times will vary between different brands of slow cookers.

3. Add the black beans to the slow cooker, stir to combine, top with the shredded chicken, and cover the slow cooker until everything is warmed through. Garnish with additional jalapeño and serve.

CHICKEN STOCK

Place 3 lbs. rinsed chicken bones in a large stockpot, cover them with water, and bring to a boil. Add 1 chopped onion, 2 chopped carrots, 3 chopped celery stalks, 3 unpeeled, smashed garlic cloves, 3 sprigs of fresh thyme, 1 teaspoon black peppercorns, 1 bay leaf, season the stock with salt, and reduce the heat so that the stock simmers. Cook for 2 hours, skimming to remove any impurities that float to the surface. Strain the stock through a fine sieve, let the stock cool slightly, and place it in the refrigerator, uncovered, to chill. Remove the fat layer and cover. The stock will keep in the refrigerator for 3 to 5 days, and in the freezer for up to 3 months.

YIELD: 4 SERVINGS   **ACTIVE TIME:** 30 MINUTES   **TOTAL TIME:** 2 HOURS AND 30 MINUTES

MOJO CHICKEN

1 yellow onion, chopped

10 garlic cloves, trimmed

2 scotch bonnet peppers, stemmed, seeds and ribs removed, and chopped

1 cup chopped fresh cilantro

1 teaspoon dried thyme

1 tablespoon cumin

½ teaspoon allspice

1 cup orange juice

½ cup fresh lemon juice

½ teaspoon citric acid

Zest and juice of 1 lime

¼ cup olive oil

Salt and pepper, to taste

2 lbs. boneless, skinless chicken breasts

1   Place all of the ingredients, except for the chicken, in a food processor or blender and puree until smooth. Reserve ½ cup of the marinade, pour the rest into a large resealable plastic bag, and add the chicken. Place in the refrigerator and marinate for 2 hours. If time allows, let the chicken marinate for up to 8 hours.

2   Remove the chicken from the refrigerator, remove it from the marinade, and pat it dry. Preheat your gas or charcoal grill to medium-high heat (about 450°F).

3   Place the chicken on the grill and cook until both sides are charred and the breasts are cooked through and springy to the touch, 4 to 5 minutes per side. Transfer the chicken to a plate and let it rest for 10 minutes.

4   While the chicken is resting, place the reserved marinade in a saucepan and bring to a simmer over medium heat, until it starts to thicken, about 10 minutes. Spoon it over the chicken and serve immediately.

YIELD: 4 SERVINGS

ACTIVE TIME: 20 MINUTES

TOTAL TIME: 2 HOURS AND 45 MINUTES

CHICKEN SOUVLAKI

10 garlic cloves, crushed

4 sprigs of fresh oregano

1 sprig of fresh rosemary

1 teaspoon paprika

1 teaspoon kosher salt

1 teaspoon black pepper

¼ cup olive oil, plus more as needed

¼ cup dry white wine

2 tablespoons fresh lemon juice

2½ lbs. boneless, skinless chicken breasts, chopped

2 bay leaves

Pita bread, warmed, for serving

Tzatziki (see sidebar), for serving

2 tomatoes, sliced, for serving

½ onion, sliced, for serving

2 cucumbers, sliced, for serving

1   Place the garlic, oregano, rosemary, paprika, salt, pepper, olive oil, wine, and lemon juice in a food processor and blitz to combine. Place the chicken and bay leaves in a bowl or a large resealable bag, pour the marinade over the chicken, and stir so that it gets evenly coated. Refrigerate for 2 hours, stirring or shaking occasionally.

2   Remove the chicken from the refrigerator, thread the pieces onto skewers, and allow them to come to room temperature. Prepare a gas or charcoal grill for medium-high heat (about 450°F).

3   Place the skewers on the grill and cook, turning frequently, until the chicken is cooked through, about 8 minutes. Remove the skewers from the grill and let them rest briefly before serving alongside the pita, Tzatziki, tomatoes, onion, and cucumbers.

TZATZIKI

Place 1 cup of plain, full-fat yogurt, ¾ cup seeded and minced cucumber, 1 minced garlic clove, and the juice of 1 lemon wedge in a mixing bowl and stir to combine. Taste and season with salt and white pepper. Stir in 2 tablespoons of finely chopped dill, place the tzatziki in the refrigerator, and chill for 1 hour before serving.

YIELD: 4 SERVINGS

ACTIVE TIME: 30 MINUTES

TOTAL TIME: 3 HOURS

BEEF SHAWARMA

3 lbs. sirloin

6 tablespoons olive oil

3 tablespoons red wine vinegar

Juice of 2 lemons

2 teaspoons cinnamon

2 tablespoons coriander

1 tablespoon black pepper

1 teaspoon cardamom

1 teaspoon ground cloves

½ teaspoon ground mace

Pinch of grated fresh nutmeg

1 tablespoon garlic powder

2 yellow onions, sliced into thin half-moons

Salt, to taste

1 teaspoon sumac powder

1 cup plain Greek yogurt, for serving

Pita bread, for serving

2 Persian cucumbers, diced, for serving

2 plum tomatoes, diced, for serving

½ cup fresh mint leaves, torn, for serving

1 Place sirloin in the freezer for 30 minutes so that it will be easier to slice. After 30 minutes, use an extremely sharp knife to slice it as thin as possible.

2 Place the sirloin in a large mixing bowl. Add the olive oil, vinegar, lemon juice, cinnamon, coriander, pepper, cardamom, cloves, mace, nutmeg, and garlic powder and stir to combine. Place in the refrigerator and let it marinate for 1 hour. If time allows, let the beef marinate overnight.

3 Place the sliced onions in a baking dish and cover with water. Add a pinch of salt and several ice cubes. Place in the refrigerator for 30 minutes.

4 Remove the meat from the refrigerator and let it come to room temperature. Drain the onions, squeeze them to remove any excess water, and place them in a bowl. Add the sumac powder and toss to coat. Set aside.

5 Warm a large cast-iron skillet over high heat. When it is warm, add the meat in batches and cook, turning as it browns, until it is browned all over, about 4 minutes per batch. To serve, place a dollop of yogurt on a pita and top with some of the meat, seasoned onions, cucumbers, tomatoes, and mint leaves.

YIELD: 4 SERVINGS

ACTIVE TIME: 15 MINUTES

TOTAL TIME: 1 HOUR

CRYING TIGER BEEF

2 lbs. flank steak

2 tablespoons soy sauce

1 tablespoon oyster sauce

1 tablespoon brown sugar, plus 1 teaspoon

1 large tomato, seeded and diced

¼ cup fresh lime juice

¼ cup fish sauce

2 tablespoons finely chopped fresh cilantro, plus more for garnish

1½ tablespoons Toasted Rice Powder (see sidebar)

1 tablespoon red pepper flakes

3 tablespoons finely chopped fresh mint, for garnish

3 tablespoons finely chopped fresh basil, for garnish

1 Place the steak in a bowl and add the soy sauce, oyster sauce, and the 1 tablespoon of brown sugar. Stir to combine and then let the steak marinate for 30 minutes.

2 Place a cast-iron skillet over high heat and spray it with nonstick cooking spray. Add the steak and cook for 4 minutes per side for medium-rare. Transfer to a plate, tent loosely with aluminum foil, and let it rest for 5 minutes before slicing into thin strips, making sure to cut against the grain.

3 Place the tomato, lime juice, fish sauce, remaining brown sugar, cilantro, Toasted Rice Powder, and red pepper flakes in a bowl and stir to combine. The powder won't dissolve, but will serve to bind the rest of the ingredients together. Divide the dipping sauce between the serving bowls, top with the slices of beef, and garnish each portion with additional cilantro, mint, and basil.

TOASTED RICE POWDER

Warm a cast-iron skillet over medium-high heat. Add ½ cup jasmine rice and toast until it starts to brown, about 4 minutes. Remove and grind into a fine powder using a mortar and pestle.

YIELD: 4 SERVINGS

ACTIVE TIME: 10 MINUTES

TOTAL TIME: 24 HOURS

RASPBERRY & TOMATO GAZPACHO

2 to 3 large heirloom tomatoes

1 cup raspberries

2 garlic cloves

½ cup peeled and diced cucumber

2 teaspoons fresh lemon juice

2 tablespoons olive oil

1 red bell pepper, stemmed, seeds and ribs removed, and chopped

Salt and pepper, to taste

Fresh mint leaves, for garnish

Heavy cream, for garnish (optional)

1 Preheat the oven to 425°F. Place the tomatoes on a baking sheet, place it in the oven, and roast until they start to collapse and their skins start to blister, about 10 to 15 minutes. Remove from the oven and let the tomatoes cool slightly.

2 Place the roasted tomatoes and the remaining ingredients, except for the garnishes, in a blender, puree until smooth, and refrigerate overnight.

3 When ready to serve, ladle the soup into bowls, season with salt and pepper, and garnish each portion with mint leaves and, if desired, approximately 1 tablespoon of heavy cream.

YIELD: 4 SERVINGS

ACTIVE TIME: 20 MINUTES

TOTAL TIME: I HOUR

HAM & SWISS STRATA

8 eggs, beaten

2 cups whole milk

4 oz. Swiss cheese, shredded

Pinch of grated fresh nutmeg

3 cups day-old bread pieces

1 cup diced cooked ham

1 yellow onion, minced

2 cups chopped spinach

Salt and pepper, to taste

2 teaspoons olive oil

1   Place the eggs and milk in a large mixing bowl and whisk to combine. Stir in the cheese and nutmeg and then add the bread pieces. Transfer the mixture to the refrigerator and chill for 30 minutes.

2   Preheat the oven to 400°F. Add the ham, onion, and spinach to the egg-and-bread mixture and stir until evenly distributed. Season with salt and pepper.

3   Coat a medium cast-iron skillet with the olive oil. Pour in the strata, place the skillet in the oven, and bake until it is golden brown and set in the center, about 25 minutes. Remove from the oven and let it rest for 10 minutes before slicing and serving.

FOR THE RICE BOWL

1 tablespoon olive oil

1 lb. extra-firm tofu, drained and chopped

2 cups day-old white rice, at room temperature

2 carrots, peeled and grated

1 cup broccoli sprouts

1 cup corn kernels

1 cup cooked edamame

Flesh from 2 avocados, sliced thin

Salt, to taste

Sesame seeds, for garnish

FOR THE DRESSING

¼ cup chopped white onion

¼ cup peanut oil

1 tablespoon rice vinegar

1-inch piece of fresh ginger, peeled and minced

1 tablespoon minced celery

1 tablespoon soy sauce

1 teaspoon tomato paste

1½ teaspoons sugar

1 teaspoon fresh lemon juice

½ teaspoon kosher salt

Black pepper, to taste

YIELD: 4 SERVINGS

ACTIVE TIME: 15 MINUTES

TOTAL TIME: 15 MINUTES

RICE BOWL WITH BENIHANA'S GINGER DRESSING

1   To begin preparations for the rice bowl, place the oil in a large skillet and warm over medium-high heat. When the oil starts to shimmer, add the tofu and cook until it is browned all over, turning the pieces as they brown, about 8 minutes.

2   To prepare the dressing, place all of the ingredients in a blender and puree until smooth.

3   Divide the rice between four bowls. Arrange the tofu, carrots, broccoli sprouts, corn, edamame, and avocados on top of the rice, sprinkle salt over the top, and drizzle the dressing over each portion. Garnish with the sesame seeds and serve.

TIP: Any protein, even fried eggs, will work in place of the tofu in this preparation.

YIELD: 6 SERVINGS

ACTIVE TIME: 15 MINUTES

TOTAL TIME: 15 MINUTES

CURRIED CHICKEN SALAD

4 cups diced cooked chicken

¼ cup mayonnaise

3 tablespoons fresh lime juice

¼ cup Madras curry powder

1 tablespoon cumin

1 tablespoon garlic powder

½ teaspoon cinnamon

½ teaspoon turmeric

Salt and pepper, to taste

3 celery stalks, minced

2 Granny Smith apples, minced

½ red bell pepper, stemmed, seeds and ribs removed, and minced

¾ cup pecans, chopped

6 oz. baby arugula, for serving (optional)

12 slices of marble rye, toasted, for serving (optional)

1   Place the chicken, mayonnaise, lime juice, and all of the seasonings in a mixing bowl and stir to combine. Add the celery, apples, red pepper, and ½ cup of the pecans and stir to incorporate.

2   Top with the remaining pecans and either serve over the arugula or use the toasted slices of marble rye to make sandwiches.

YIELD: 8 SERVINGS

ACTIVE TIME: 15 MINUTES

TOTAL TIME: 25 MINUTES

PORK FRIED RICE

¼ cup olive oil

1-inch piece of fresh ginger, peeled and minced

2 garlic cloves, minced

3 large eggs

2 carrots, peeled and minced

4 cups day-old white rice

4 scallions, trimmed and chopped

1 cup peas

2 tablespoons soy sauce

1 tablespoon rice vinegar

1 tablespoon fish sauce

1 tablespoon sesame oil

2 cups chopped leftover pork tenderloin

1   Place the oil in a 12-inch cast-iron skillet and warm over medium-high heat. When the oil starts to shimmer, add the ginger and garlic and cook until they just start to brown, about 2 minutes.

2   Add the eggs and scramble until they are set, about 2 minutes. Stir in the carrots, rice, scallions, peas, soy sauce, rice vinegar, fish sauce, sesame oil, and pork and cook, stirring constantly, until the pork is warmed through, about 5 minutes. Serve immediately.

YIELD: 4 SERVINGS

ACTIVE TIME: 20 MINUTES

TOTAL TIME: 30 MINUTES

CHICKEN & COCONUT WITH CUCUMBER NOODLES

2 tablespoons olive oil

3 chicken breasts

5 large cucumbers, peeled, halved lengthwise, and seeded

½ cup shredded unsweetened coconut

Zest and juice from 2 limes

¼ cup coconut milk

1 teaspoon chili garlic sauce, plus more as needed

½-inch piece of fresh ginger, peeled and grated

1 teaspoon sugar

1 teaspoon cumin

1 teaspoon kosher salt, plus more to taste

6 scallions, trimmed and sliced thin, for garnish

½ cup roasted peanuts, chopped, for garnish

1 Place the olive oil in a large skillet and warm over medium heat. When the oil starts to shimmer, add the chicken breasts and cook until browned, cooked through, and springy to the touch, about 5 minutes per side. Remove the chicken from the pan and let it rest for 10 minutes. When the chicken is cool enough to handle, shred it with a fork.

2 Quarter each cucumber half and then cut the quarters into ⅛-inch-wide strips. Place them on paper towels to drain.

3 Place the coconut, lime juice, coconut milk, chili garlic sauce, ginger, sugar, cumin, and salt in a small food processor or a blender and puree until smooth.

4 Place the cucumber strips and chicken in a large serving bowl. Add the coconut mixture and toss to coat.

5 Sprinkle the lime zest, scallions, and peanuts on top of the dressed salad, season to taste, and serve.

FOR THE AIOLI

1 cup sun-dried tomatoes in olive oil, drained and chopped

1 cup mayonnaise

1 tablespoon whole grain mustard

2 tablespoons finely chopped fresh parsley

2 tablespoons minced scallions

1 teaspoon white balsamic vinegar

1 garlic clove, minced

2 teaspoons kosher salt

1 teaspoon black pepper

FOR THE SANDWICHES

8 slices of sourdough bread

8 slices of cheddar cheese

4 cooked chicken breasts, sliced

12 strips of crispy bacon

1 cup arugula

YIELD: 4 SERVINGS

ACTIVE TIME: 30 MINUTES

TOTAL TIME: 30 MINUTES

CHICKEN PANINIS WITH SUN-DRIED TOMATO AIOLI

1 Preheat a panini press. To prepare the aioli, place all of the ingredients in a mixing bowl and stir until combined.

2 To begin preparations for the sandwiches, spread some of the aioli on each slice of bread. Place a slice of cheddar on each slice of bread. Divide the chicken between four slices of the bread. Top each portion of chicken with 3 slices of bacon and ¼ cup of the arugula. Assemble the sandwiches with the other slices of bread.

3 Place the sandwiches in the panini press and press until the cheese has melted and there is a nicely browned crust on the bread. Remove and serve immediately.

NOTE: If you don't have a panini press, don't worry. Warm a cast-iron skillet in the oven. Place I tablespoon of olive oil in another skillet and warm over medium-high heat. When the oil starts to shimmer, place a sandwich in the pan, place the warm cast-iron skillet on top so it is pressing down on the sandwich, and cook until golden brown. Turn the sandwich over and repeat.

YIELD: 4 SERVINGS

ACTIVE TIME: 30 MINUTES

TOTAL TIME: 30 MINUTES

FISH & CHIPS

4 cups canola oil

5 potatoes, sliced into long, thin strips

3 tablespoons finely chopped fresh rosemary

Salt, to taste

2 eggs, beaten

1 cup cornmeal

1½ lbs. pollock fillets

1   Place the oil in a deep, heavy bottomed pot and bring to 350°F over medium-high heat.

2   When the oil is ready, place the sliced potatoes in the oil and cook until golden brown. Remove the fried potatoes and transfer to a paper towel–lined plate to drain. Heat the oil back to 350°F.

3   Place the fried potatoes in a bowl with the rosemary and salt and toss to coat. Set them aside.

4   Place the beaten eggs in a small bowl and the cornmeal in another. Dip the pollock fillets in the egg and then in the cornmeal, repeating until they are coated all over. Place the battered pollock in the oil and fry until golden brown and cooked through, 5 to 7 minutes. Remove and set to drain and cool on another paper towel–lined plate. Serve with the fried potatoes.

PICKLED RAMPS

Place ½ cup champagne vinegar, ½ cup water, ¼ cup sugar, 1½ teaspoons kosher salt, ¼ teaspoon fennel seeds, ¼ teaspoon coriander seeds, and ⅛ teaspoon red pepper flakes in a small saucepan and bring to a boil. Add 10 small ramp bulbs, reduce heat, and simmer for 1 minute. Transfer the contents of the saucepan to a mason jar, cover, and let cool completely before using or storing. The ramps will keep in the refrigerator for up to 1 week.

FOR THE SALAD

Salt and pepper, to taste

1 small head of cauliflower, trimmed and chopped

1 head of broccoli, cut into florets

¼ cup olive oil

4 oz. Brussels sprouts, trimmed and halved

Pickled Ramps (see sidebar)

Parmesan cheese, grated, for garnish

Red pepper flakes, for garnish

FOR THE DRESSING

2 garlic cloves, minced

1 teaspoon miso paste

⅔ cup mayonnaise

¼ cup buttermilk

¼ cup grated Parmesan cheese

Zest of 1 lemon

1 teaspoon Worcestershire sauce

1 teaspoon kosher salt, plus more to taste

½ teaspoon black pepper, plus more to taste

YIELD: 4 SERVINGS

ACTIVE TIME: 20 MINUTES

TOTAL TIME: 45 MINUTES

CHARRED BRASSICA SALAD WITH BUTTERMILK CAESAR

1   To begin preparations for the salad, bring a large pot of water to a boil. Add salt and the cauliflower, cook for 1 minute, remove the cauliflower with a slotted spoon, and transfer to a paper towel–lined plate. Wait for the water to return to a boil, add the broccoli, and cook for 30 seconds. Use a slotted spoon to remove the broccoli and transfer it to the paper towel–lined plate.

2   Place the oil and Brussels sprouts, cut side down, in a large cast-iron skillet. Add the broccoli and cauliflower, season with salt and pepper, and cook over high heat, making sure not to move the vegetables, until charred. Turn the vegetables over and cook until

charred on that side. Remove the mixture from the pan and transfer it to a salad bowl.

3   To prepare the dressing, place the garlic, miso, mayonnaise, buttermilk, Parmesan cheese, lemon zest, Worcestershire sauce, salt, and pepper in a food processor and blitz until combined. Taste and adjust the seasoning if necessary.

4   Add the Pickled Ramps and dressing to the salad bowl and toss to evenly coat. Garnish with Parmesan cheese and red pepper flakes and serve.

YIELD: 4 SERVINGS

ACTIVE TIME: 25 MINUTES

TOTAL TIME: 45 MINUTES

CHILI-DUSTED CAULIFLOWER & CHICKPEA SALAD

FOR THE SALAD

1 (14 oz.) can of chickpeas, drained and rinsed

3 cups cauliflower florets, chopped

3 garlic cloves, sliced thin

1 shallot, sliced thin

⅓ cup olive oil

½ teaspoon chili powder

½ teaspoon chipotle chili powder

½ teaspoon black pepper

½ teaspoon onion powder

½ teaspoon garlic powder

¼ teaspoon paprika

1 tablespoon kosher salt

FOR THE DRESSING

2 scallions, trimmed and sliced thin

2 Fresno chili peppers, stemmed, seeds and ribs removed, and sliced thin

3 tablespoons sugar

¼ cup red wine vinegar

½ teaspoon dark chili powder

½ teaspoon chipotle chili powder

½ teaspoon black pepper

½ teaspoon onion powder

½ teaspoon garlic powder

¼ teaspoon paprika

½ tablespoon kosher salt

1   Preheat the oven to 400°F. To prepare the salad, place all of the ingredients in a mixing bowl and toss to coat. Place the mixture in a 9 x 13–inch baking pan, place the pan in the oven, and roast until the cauliflower is slightly charred and still crunchy, about 30 minutes. Remove from the oven and let the mixture cool slightly.

2   To prepare the dressing, place all of the ingredients in a food processor and blitz until combined. Transfer the dressing to a salad bowl, add the cooked cauliflower-and-chickpea mixture in the bowl, toss to coat, and serve.

YIELD: 6 SERVINGS

ACTIVE TIME: 10 MINUTES

TOTAL TIME: 5 HOURS

SPINACH & MUSHROOM QUINOA

1½ cups quinoa, rinsed

2½ cups Vegetable Stock (see page 22)

1 yellow onion, chopped

½ red bell pepper, stemmed, seeds and ribs removed, and chopped

¾ lb. portobello mushrooms, chopped

2 garlic cloves, minced

1 tablespoon kosher salt, plus more to taste

1 tablespoon black pepper, plus more to taste

3 cups baby spinach

1½ cups fresh basil leaves, chopped

¼ cup finely chopped fresh dill

2 tablespoons finely chopped fresh thyme

1   Place all of the ingredients, except for the spinach and fresh herbs, in a slow cooker and cook on high until the quinoa is tender and slightly fluffy, about 4 hours.

2   Add the spinach and turn off the heat. Keep the slow cooker covered and let the mixture sit for 1 hour.

3   Fluff the quinoa with a fork, add the basil, dill, and thyme, and fold to incorporate. Season with salt and pepper and serve.

YIELD: 4 SERVINGS

ACTIVE TIME: 20 MINUTES

TOTAL TIME: 45 MINUTES

MISO RAMEN WITH SPICY BEAN SPROUT SALAD

1   To prepare the salad, bring water to a boil in a small saucepan. Add the bean sprouts and cook for 2 minutes. Drain and let cool. Place the remaining ingredients in a salad bowl and stir to combine. Add the cooled bean sprouts, gently stir to incorporate, and set the salad aside.

2   To begin preparations for the ramen, place the sesame seeds in a dry skillet and toast over medium heat until browned, about 2 minutes. Remove the sesame seeds from the pan and use a mortar and pestle to grind them into a paste, adding water as needed.

3   Place the sesame oil in a large saucepan and warm over medium heat. When the oil starts to shimmer, add the garlic, ginger, and shallots and cook until fragrant, about 2 minutes.

4   Raise the heat to medium-high and add the chili garlic sauce, miso, toasted sesame paste, sugar, sake, and stock and stir to combine. Bring to a boil, reduce heat so that the soup simmers, and season with salt and pepper. Simmer for about 5 minutes and remove from heat.

5   While the soup is simmering, cook the noodles according to the manufacturer's instructions. Drain the noodles and place them in warmed bowls. Pour the soup over the noodles and top each portion with the bean sprout salad.

TIP: If you're looking to add some substance to this ramen, top each portion with a poached egg. If you want to make it even heartier, thinly sliced chicken or beef will work wonderfully with the broth.

FOR THE SALAD

¾ lb. bean sprouts

1 tablespoon sesame seeds

2 scallions, trimmed and sliced thin

2 tablespoons sesame oil

2 teaspoons soy sauce

⅛ teaspoon red pepper flakes

Pinch of ground ginger

Zest of 1 orange

FOR THE RAMEN

¼ cup sesame seeds

2 tablespoons sesame oil

4 garlic cloves, minced

2-inch piece of fresh ginger, peeled and minced

2 shallots, minced

2 teaspoons chili garlic sauce

6 tablespoons white miso paste

2 tablespoons sugar

2 tablespoons sake

8 cups Vegetable Stock (see page 22)

Salt and pepper, to taste

Noodles from 2 packages of Ramen

Pickled red ginger, for garnish

YIELD: 4 SERVINGS

 ACTIVE TIME: 30 MINUTES

 TOTAL TIME: 3 HOURS

STEAK WITH PEPPERS & ONIONS

½ cup olive oil

2 garlic cloves, minced

2 teaspoons Worcestershire sauce

2 teaspoons red wine vinegar

1 tablespoon mustard powder

2 lbs. sirloin tips, chopped

2 yellow onions, chopped

2 red bell peppers, stemmed, seeds and ribs removed, and chopped

Salt and pepper, to taste

1 Place 7 tablespoons of the oil in a large bowl. Add the garlic, Worcestershire sauce, red wine vinegar, and mustard powder and stir to combine. Add the sirloin tips and stir until they are coated. Cover and refrigerate for 2 hours, while stirring once or twice. If time allows, let the sirloin tips marinate overnight.

2 Approximately 30 minutes before you are ready to cook, remove the sirloin tips from the marinade and allow them to come to room temperature.

3 Place a 12-inch cast-iron skillet over medium-high heat and coat the bottom with the remaining oil. When it starts to shimmer, add the sirloin tips and cook until they are browned all over, about 8 minutes. Remove from the pan and set aside.

4 Reduce the heat to medium, add the onions and peppers, and cook, without stirring, until they are browned, about 5 minutes. Return the sirloin tips to the pan and cook for an additional 2 minutes. Season with salt and pepper and serve immediately.

TIP: This dish is also a great make-ahead dish, served cold in crusty rolls and topped with arugula.

YIELD: 6 SERVINGS

ACTIVE TIME: 20 MINUTES

TOTAL TIME: 40 MINUTES

VEGGIE LO MEIN

¼ cup sesame oil

3 tablespoons soy sauce

2 tablespoons black vinegar

1 tablespoon brown sugar

3 tablespoons fish sauce

1 tablespoon olive oil

6 scallions, trimmed and chopped

1-inch piece of fresh ginger, peeled and minced

2 garlic cloves, minced

1½ cups button mushrooms, sliced

½ white onion, sliced

½ cup bean sprouts

1 carrot, peeled and julienned

1 lb. lo mein noodles

1   Place the sesame oil, soy sauce, black vinegar, brown sugar, and fish sauce in a mixing bowl, stir to combine, and set the mixture aside.

2   Place the olive oil, scallion whites, ginger, and garlic in a Dutch oven and cook over high heat for 2 minutes. Add the mushrooms, onion, bean sprouts, and carrot and cook until the vegetables are cooked through but still crisp, about 4 minutes. Remove the mixture from the pan and set aside to cool.

3   Wipe out the pot, fill it with water, and bring to a boil. Add the noodles and cook until al dente, about 6 minutes. Drain and add the noodles to the mixing bowl containing the sesame oil-and-soy sauce dressing. Toss to coat, add the vegetables and the scallion greens, and toss to combine. Serve immediately or refrigerate for up to 2 days.

YIELD: 4 SERVINGS

ACTIVE TIME: 15 MINUTES

TOTAL TIME: 2 HOURS AND 30 MINUTES

GRILLED TUNA STEAKS WITH WASABI BUTTER

FOR THE WASABI BUTTER

1 stick of unsalted butter, at room temperature

1 teaspoon prepared wasabi

½ teaspoon kosher salt

¼ teaspoon soy sauce

FOR THE TUNA

4 tuna steaks (each about 2 inches thick)

2 tablespoons olive oil, plus more as needed

1 tablespoon black pepper

1 tablespoon kosher salt

1   To prepare the wasabi butter, place all of ingredients in a bowl and stir until thoroughly combined. Cover the bowl with aluminum foil and refrigerate for at least 2 hours before serving.

2   To begin preparations for the tuna, rub the tuna steaks with a little olive oil and then season with the pepper and salt. Let stand at room temperature. Preheat your gas or charcoal grill to high heat (about 500°F).

3   Brush the grates with a little olive oil. Tuna steaks should always be cooked between rare and medium-rare; anything more will make them tough and dry. Place the tuna steaks directly over the hottest part of the grill and cook for about 2 minutes per side.

4   Transfer the tuna steaks to a cutting board and let them rest for 5 to 10 minutes. Slice against the grain and serve with the wasabi butter.

YIELD: 4 SERVINGS

ACTIVE TIME: 15 MINUTES

TOTAL TIME: 25 MINUTES

HUEVOS RANCHEROS

2 tablespoons olive oil

4 Corn Tortillas (see sidebar)

1 (14 oz.) can of black beans, drained and rinsed

1 tablespoon unsalted butter

8 eggs

½ cup grated sharp cheddar cheese

½ cup crumbled Cotija cheese or grated Monterey Jack cheese

2 jalapeño peppers, stemmed, seeds and ribs removed, and sliced, for garnish

Fresh cilantro, finely chopped, for garnish

Salsa, for serving

1   Place the olive oil in a large cast-iron skillet and warm over medium-high heat. When the oil starts to shimmer, add the tortillas and cook until they start to brown. Add the beans and butter and mash the beans into the tortillas. Cook until the beans are warmed through, about 2 minutes.

2   Break the eggs over the beans, cover the skillet, and cook until the whites start to set, about 2 minutes.

3   Remove the lid, top with the cheeses, garnish with the jalapeños and cilantro, and serve with salsa.

CORN TORTILLAS

Place 2 cups masa harina and ½ teaspoon kosher salt in a bowl and stir to combine. Slowly add 1 cup of warm water (110°F) and 2 tablespoons of vegetable oil and stir until they are incorporated and a soft dough forms. The dough should be quite soft and not at all sticky. If it is too dry, add more water. If the dough is too wet, add more masa harina. Wrap the dough in plastic and let it rest at room temperature for 30 minutes.

Warm a cast-iron skillet over medium-high heat. Pinch off a small piece of the dough and roll it into a ball. Place the ball between two pieces of parchment paper or plastic wrap and use a large cookbook (or something of similar weight) to flatten the ball into a thin disk. Place the disk in the skillet and cook until brown spots begin to appear, about 45 seconds. Flip the disk over, cook for 1 minute, and transfer the cooked tortilla to a plate. Cover with a kitchen towel and repeat with the remaining dough.

YIELD: 6 SERVINGS

ACTIVE TIME: 40 MINUTES

TOTAL TIME: 50 MINUTES

COUSCOUS & SHRIMP SALAD

¾ lb. shrimp, peeled and deveined

6 bunches of fresh mint

10 garlic cloves, peeled

3½ cups Chicken Stock (see page 37)

3 cups Israeli couscous

1 bunch of asparagus, trimmed

3 plum tomatoes, diced

1 tablespoon finely chopped fresh oregano

½ English cucumber, diced

Zest and juice of 1 lemon

½ cup diced red onion

½ cup sun-dried tomatoes in olive oil, sliced thin

¼ cup pitted and chopped Kalamata olives

⅓ cup olive oil

Salt and pepper, to taste

½ cup crumbled feta cheese

1   Place the shrimp, mint, and garlic in a Dutch oven and cover with water. Bring to a simmer over medium heat and cook until the shrimp are pink and cooked through, about 5 minutes after the water comes to a simmer. Drain, cut the shrimp in half lengthwise, and them set aside. Discard the mint and garlic cloves.

2   Place the stock in the Dutch oven and bring to a boil. Add the couscous, reduce the heat so that the stock simmers, cover, and cook until the couscous is tender and has absorbed the stock, 7 to 10 minutes. Transfer the couscous to a salad bowl.

3   Fill the pot with water and bring it to a boil. Add the asparagus and cook until it has softened, 1 to 1½ minutes. Drain, rinse under cold water, and chop into bite-sized pieces. Pat the asparagus dry.

4   Add all of the remaining ingredients, except for the feta, to the salad bowl containing the couscous. Add the asparagus and stir to incorporate. Top with the shrimp and the feta and serve.

YIELD: 4 SERVINGS

ACTIVE TIME: 15 MINUTES

TOTAL TIME: 30 MINUTES

SPAGHETTI ALLA CARBONARA

2½ tablespoons olive oil

4 oz. bacon, diced

Salt and pepper, to taste

2 large eggs, at room temperature

¾ cup grated Parmesan cheese, plus more for garnish

1 lb. spaghetti

1   Bring a large saucepan of water to a boil. While the water comes to a boil, heat a medium skillet over medium-low heat for 2 to 3 minutes. Add 2 tablespoons of the olive oil to the skillet and let it warm for a couple of minutes. Raise the heat to medium, add the bacon, and season it with pepper. Cook, while stirring occasionally, until the bacon renders its fat and starts turning golden brown, about 6 minutes. Remove the skillet from heat and partially cover it.

2   Place the eggs in a small bowl and whisk until scrambled. Add the Parmesan, season with salt and pepper, and whisk until combined.

3   Once the water is boiling, add salt and the pasta. Cook 2 minutes short of the directed cooking time, so that the pasta is soft but still quite firm. Reserve ¼ cup of the pasta water and then drain the pasta.

4   Return the pot to the stove, raise the heat to high, and add the remaining olive oil and the reserved pasta water. Add the drained pasta and toss. Remove the pot from heat, add the bacon and the egg-and-Parmesan mixture, and toss to coat the pasta. Divide the pasta between four warm bowls, season with pepper, and top with additional Parmesan.

PORTS
IN A
STORM

It is almost guaranteed that there will be at least one time a week where consuming something comforting is required. If that need happens to arise on a weeknight, the tendency is to reach for a takeout menu, or swing by the store to procure one of the numerous junky, processed items on offer. The issue: both of these options often result in the individual who needs some solace actually feeling worse.

As a valley or two are inevitable, we figured it would be best to provide a series of preparations that could soothe and still be prepared after the demands of a difficult day have sapped most of your energy. It's not an easy balance to strike, but, knowing how important a charge it is, we believe you'll agree that we've managed it quite well.

ROMESCO SAUCE

Place 2 large roasted red bell peppers, 1 smashed garlic clove, ½ cup slivered and toasted almonds, ¼ cup pureed tomatoes, 2 tablespoons finely chopped fresh parsley, 2 tablespoons sherry vinegar, and 1 teaspoon smoked paprika in a food processor and blitz until smooth. With the food processor running, gradually incorporate ½ cup olive oil into the sauce. Season with salt and pepper and use as desired.

2 tablespoons olive oil

½ small red onion, chopped

2 garlic cloves, minced

1 large egg

2 tablespoons whole milk

½ cup Italian bread crumbs

¼ cup grated Parmesan cheese

2 tablespoons finely chopped fresh parsley

3 tablespoons minced dried currants

2 tablespoons finely chopped fresh oregano

¼ cup pine nuts, toasted

¾ lb. ground pork

½ lb. sweet or spicy ground Italian sausage

Salt and pepper, to taste

2 cups Romesco Sauce (see sidebar)

YIELD: 4 SERVINGS

ACTIVE TIME: 20 MINUTES

TOTAL TIME: 45 MINUTES

SICILIAN MEATBALLS

1 Preheat the broiler to high, position a rack so that the tops of the meatballs will be approximately 6 inches below the broiler, and line a rimmed baking sheet with aluminum foil.

2 Place the olive oil in a large skillet and warm over medium-high heat. When it starts to shimmer, add the onion and garlic and sauté until the onion is translucent, about 3 minutes. Remove the pan from heat and set it aside.

3 Place the egg, milk, bread crumbs, Parmesan, parsley, currants, oregano, and pine nuts in a mixing bowl and stir until combined. Add the pork, sausage, and onion mixture, season with salt and pepper, and stir until thoroughly combined. Working with wet hands, form the mixture into 1½-inch meatballs, arrange them on the baking sheet, and spray the tops with cooking spray.

4 Place the meatballs in the oven and broil until browned all over, turning them as they cook. Remove the meatballs from the oven and set them aside.

5 Place the sauce in the skillet and warm over medium heat. Add the meatballs to the sauce, reduce the heat to low, cover the pan, and simmer, turning the meatballs occasionally, until they are cooked through, about 15 minutes. Season with salt and pepper and serve.

TIP: As you might expect of a sauce that originated in the coastal villages of Catalonia, the Romesco Sauce is wonderful with a wide range of seafood.

YIELD: 4 SERVINGS

ACTIVE TIME: 30 MINUTES

TOTAL TIME: I HOUR AND 20 MINUTES

STUFFED EGGPLANTS

2 large eggplants, halved

2 tablespoons olive oil, plus more as needed

½ cup quinoa, rinsed

1 cup water

2 onions, chopped

3 garlic cloves, minced

2 bell peppers, stemmed, seeds and ribs removed, and chopped

1 lb. ground lamb

Salt and pepper, to taste

½ teaspoon garam masala

2 teaspoons cumin

Fresh parsley, finely chopped, for garnish

1   Preheat the oven to 400°F. Place the eggplants on a baking sheet, drizzle olive oil over the top, and place them in the oven. Roast until the flesh is tender, about 30 minutes. Remove from the oven and let the eggplants cool slightly. When cool enough to handle, scoop out the flesh, mince it, and place it in a mixing bowl. Set the hollowed-out eggplants aside and leave the oven on.

2   Place the quinoa and water in a saucepan and bring to a boil over medium heat. Let the quinoa boil until it has absorbed all of the water. Remove the pan from heat, cover it, and let it steam for 5 minutes. Fluff with a fork and let cool slightly.

3   Place the olive oil in a large skillet and warm it over medium-high heat. When the oil starts to shimmer, add the onions, garlic, and bell peppers and sauté until the onions and peppers start to soften, about 5 minutes. Add the ground lamb, season it with salt and pepper, stir in the garam masala and cumin, and cook, breaking the lamb up with a fork, until it is browned, about 6 minutes. Transfer the mixture to the bowl containing the minced eggplant. Add the quinoa to the bowl and stir until the mixture is combined.

4   Fill the cavities of the hollowed-out eggplants with the lamb-and-quinoa mixture. Place them on a baking sheet, place them in the oven, and roast until they are starting to collapse, about 15 minutes. Remove from the oven and let them cool slightly before garnishing with the parsley and serving.

3 lbs. potatoes, peeled and chopped

1 garlic clove, minced

2 teaspoons kosher salt

1 teaspoon black pepper

1 tablespoon olive oil

1 small green bell pepper, seeded and minced

1 yellow onion, minced

½ lb. ground beef

2 tablespoons tomato paste

¼ cup pitted and sliced green olives

¼ cup raisins

½ teaspoon paprika

Vegetable oil, as needed

2 eggs, lightly beaten

½ cup bread crumbs

YIELD: 4 SERVINGS

ACTIVE TIME: 30 MINUTES

TOTAL TIME: I HOUR

PAPAS RELLENAS

1   Bring water to a boil in a large saucepan. Add the potatoes, cover the pan, and cook until the potatoes are fork-tender, about 25 minutes. Drain the potatoes, place them in a large bowl, and mash until smooth. Add the garlic and half of the salt and pepper and stir to incorporate.

2   Warm the olive oil in a skillet over medium heat. When the oil starts to shimmer, add the bell pepper and onion and sauté until the onion is translucent, about 3 minutes. Add the ground beef and cook, breaking it up with a fork, until it is browned, about 8 minutes. Stir in the tomato paste, olives, raisins, paprika, and the remaining salt and pepper and cook for 2 minutes. Transfer the mixture to a paper towel–lined baking sheet and let it drain.

3   Add vegetable oil to a Dutch oven until it is 2 inches deep and bring it to 375°F. Place the eggs and bread crumbs in two separate bowls. Place 2 tablespoons of the potato mixture in one hand, pat it down until it is flat, and then place a tablespoon of the ground beef mixture in the center. Shape the potato around the filling to create a ball and dip the ball into the egg. Roll the ball in the bread crumbs until coated and place on a parchment–lined baking sheet. Repeat until all of the potato mixture and ground beef mixture have been used up.

4   Carefully place the balls in the hot oil and deep-fry until golden brown, about 2 minutes. Remove with a slotted spoon and set them on a paper towel–lined plate to drain. When all of the balls have been fried, serve with your favorite condiments and sauces.

YIELD: 4 SERVINGS

ACTIVE TIME: 20 MINUTES

TOTAL TIME: 45 MINUTES

AFRICAN PEANUT & QUINOA SOUP

1 tablespoon olive oil

1 tablespoon unsalted butter

1 red onion, chopped

½ sweet potato, peeled and chopped

1 green bell pepper, stemmed, seeds and ribs removed, and chopped

2 celery stalks, chopped

1 zucchini, chopped

1 jalapeño pepper, stemmed, seeds and ribs removed, and minced

1 garlic clove, minced

6 cups Vegetable Stock (see page 22)

¾ cup quinoa, rinsed

1 teaspoon cumin

½ cup peanut butter

Salt and pepper, to taste

Fresh oregano, finely chopped, for garnish

Peanuts, toasted, for garnish

1   Place the oil and butter in a large saucepan and warm over medium heat. When the butter has melted, add the red onion, sweet potato, bell pepper, celery, zucchini, jalapeño, and garlic and cook until the vegetables are soft, about 10 minutes.

2   Add the stock and bring the soup to a boil. Reduce the heat so that the soup simmers, stir in the quinoa and cumin, cover, and simmer until the quinoa is tender, about 15 minutes.

3   Stir in the peanut butter and season the soup with salt and pepper. Ladle into warmed bowls and garnish with the oregano and toasted peanuts.

YIELD: 4 SERVINGS

ACTIVE TIME: 15 MINUTES

TOTAL TIME: 45 MINUTES

MEDITERRANEAN CHICKEN BAKE

2 lbs. boneless, skinless chicken breasts, halved along their equators

Salt and pepper, to taste

1 tablespoon finely chopped fresh oregano

1 teaspoon finely chopped fresh thyme

1 teaspoon paprika

4 garlic cloves, minced

3 tablespoons olive oil, plus more as needed

Juice of ½ lemon

1 red onion, sliced thin

1 lb. tomatoes, sliced

Fresh basil leaves, for garnish

Fresh parsley, finely chopped, for garnish

1   Preheat the oven to 425°F. Place the chicken breasts in a bowl, season with salt and pepper, and then add the oregano, thyme, paprika, garlic, olive oil, and lemon juice. Stir until the chicken is evenly coated and set it aside.

2   Coat the bottom of a baking dish with olive oil and then distribute the red onion over it. Place the chicken breasts on top, arrange the tomato slices on top, and cover the baking dish with aluminum foil.

3   Place the dish in the oven and roast for 10 minutes. Remove the foil and bake for another 5 to 7 minutes, until the chicken is cooked through. Remove from the oven and let rest for 10 minutes before garnishing with the basil and parsley.

YIELD: 2 PIZZAS

ACTIVE TIME: 45 MINUTES

TOTAL TIME: 9 HOURS

NEW YORK-STYLE PIZZA

⅛ teaspoon instant yeast

10.9 oz. bread flour or "00" flour, plus more as needed

6.75 oz. water

1½ teaspoons table salt

Olive oil, as needed

Semolina flour, as needed

1 cup Marinara Sauce (see page 115)

3 cups shredded mozzarella cheese

Dried oregano, to taste

1 In a large bowl, combine the yeast, flour, and water. Work the mixture until it just holds together. Dust a work surface with either bread or "00" flour and knead the dough until it is compact, smooth, and elastic.

2 Add the salt and knead until the dough is developed and elastic, meaning it pulls back when stretched. Transfer the dough to an airtight container and let it rest at room temperature for 2 hours.

3 Divide the dough into two pieces and shape them into very tight balls. Place the balls of dough in a baking dish with high edges, leaving enough space between rounds that they won't touch when fully risen. Cover with oiled plastic wrap and let them rest until they have doubled in size, about 6 hours.

4 Place a baking stone on the middle rack of your oven and preheat the oven to the maximum temperature. Dust a work surface with semolina flour, place the balls of dough on the surface, and gently stretch them into 10- to 12-inch rounds. Cover them with the sauce and top with the mozzarella. Season with oregano and drizzle olive oil over the pizzas.

5 Using a peel or a flat baking sheet, transfer one pizza at a time to the heated baking stone in the oven. Bake for about 15 minutes, until the crust is golden brown and starting to char. Remove, repeat with the other pizza, and let both cool slightly before serving.

YIELD: 4 SERVINGS

ACTIVE TIME: 20 MINUTES

TOTAL TIME: 1 HOUR AND 45 MINUTES

DAL

2 tablespoons olive oil

1 yellow onion, chopped

2 garlic cloves, minced

2 teaspoons red pepper flakes

2 curry leaves (optional)

1 teaspoon kosher salt

1½ cups yellow split peas, sorted and rinsed

4 cups water

1 teaspoon turmeric

1 cup fresh peas

1   Place the olive oil in a Dutch oven and warm it over medium-high heat. When the oil starts to shimmer, add the onion, garlic, red pepper flakes, curry leaves (if using), and salt and sauté until the onion is translucent, about 3 minutes.

2   Add the yellow split peas, water, and turmeric and bring the mixture to a simmer. Cover and gently simmer for 1 hour, stirring two or three times.

3   Remove the lid and simmer, while stirring occasionally, until the dal has thickened, about 30 minutes. When the dal has the consistency of porridge, stir in the fresh peas and cook until they are warmed through. Ladle the dal into warmed bowls and serve.

YIELD: 6 SERVINGS   **ACTIVE TIME:** 40 MINUTES   **TOTAL TIME:** 3 HOURS AND 30 MINUTES

BEEF & PORK BURGERS

1 lb. ground beef

1 lb. ground pork

Salt and pepper, to taste

2 tablespoons unsalted butter

2 sweet onions, sliced thin

½ cup mayonnaise

6 brioche buns, toasted

6 slices of preferred cheese

1   Place the beef and pork in a mixing bowl and season with salt and pepper. Stir to combine, cover, and place it in the refrigerator.

2   Place the butter in a skillet and melt over medium-low heat.

3   Add the onions and a pinch of salt and cook, while stirring frequently, until the onions develop a deep brown color, about 20 to 30 minutes. Remove the pan from heat and let the onions cool completely.

4   Transfer the cooled onions to a food processor and blitz until smooth. Place the puree and mayonnaise in a mixing bowl, season with salt and pepper, and stir to combine. Place the mixture in the refrigerator for 2 hours.

5   When ready to serve, preheat a grill to 450°F or place a cast-iron skillet over medium-high heat. Divide the beef-and-pork mixture into 6 balls and then gently shape them into patties.

6   Place the burgers on the grill or in the skillet and cook for 8 to 10 minutes. Flip the burgers over and cook until cooked through, about 5 to 8 minutes. Since you are working with pork, it is important to cook the burgers all the way through. If you're worried that they will dry out, don't fret. The pork fat will keep the burgers moist and flavorful.

7   Spread the mayonnaise on one half of a bun. Place a burger on another half of the toasted buns, top with slices of cheese, and assemble.

YIELD: 6 SERVINGS

ACTIVE TIME: 30 MINUTES

TOTAL TIME: 1 HOUR AND 45 MINUTES

COTTAGE PIE

6 russet potatoes, peeled and chopped

½ teaspoon kosher salt, plus more to taste

1 stick of unsalted butter, divided into tablespoons

½ cup whole milk

¼ cup plain yogurt

Black pepper, to taste

1 tablespoon olive oil

½ yellow onion, minced

1 lb. ground beef

2 cups frozen peas

1 cup corn kernels

1   Preheat the oven to 350°F. Place the potato pieces in a large saucepan or pot and cover with cold water. Add the salt and bring the water to a boil. Reduce heat so that the water simmers and cook the potatoes until fork-tender, about 20 minutes.

2   Drain the potatoes and place them in a large bowl. Add 6 tablespoons of the butter, the milk, and yogurt and mash the potatoes until smooth. Season with salt and pepper and set aside.

3   Place the olive oil in a large cast-iron skillet and warm it over medium heat. When the oil starts to shimmer, add the onion and sauté until translucent, about 3 minutes. Add the ground beef and cook, while breaking it up with a fork, until browned, about 8 minutes. Drain the fat from the skillet, stir in the peas and corn, and season with salt and pepper.

4   Spread the mashed potatoes over the meat and vegetables and use a rubber spatula to smooth the top. Cut the remaining butter into slivers and dot the potatoes with them.

5   Cover the skillet with aluminum foil, place it in the oven, and bake for 30 minutes. Remove the foil and bake for another 10 minutes, until the potatoes start to turn golden brown. Remove from the oven and let cool for 5 minutes before serving.

YIELD: 4 SERVINGS

ACTIVE TIME: 20 MINUTES

TOTAL TIME: 1 HOUR

EGGPLANT PARMESAN

1 large eggplant

Salt, to taste

2 tablespoons olive oil

1 cup Italian bread crumbs

½ cup grated Parmesan cheese

1 egg, beaten

Marinara Sauce (see page 115), as needed

2 garlic cloves, minced

½ lb. shredded mozzarella cheese

Fresh basil, finely chopped, for serving

1 Preheat the oven to 350°F. Trim the top and bottom from the eggplant and slice it into ¼-inch-thick slices. Put the slices on paper towels in a single layer, sprinkle salt over them, and let rest for about 15 minutes. Turn the slices over, salt the other side, and let them rest for another 15 minutes. Rinse the eggplant and pat dry with paper towels.

2 Drizzle the oil over a baking sheet. In a shallow bowl, combine the bread crumbs and Parmesan cheese. Put the beaten egg in another shallow bowl. Dip the slices of eggplant in the egg and then in the bread crumb-and-cheese mixture until both sides are coated. Place the breaded slices on the baking sheet.

3 When all of the eggplant has been breaded, place it in the oven and bake for 10 minutes. Remove, turn the slices over, and bake for another 10 minutes. Remove the eggplant from the oven and let it cool slightly.

4 Place a layer of sauce in a square 8-inch baking dish or a cast-iron skillet and stir in the garlic. Lay some of the eggplant slices on top of the sauce, top them with more sauce, and then arrange the remaining eggplant on top. Sprinkle the mozzarella over the eggplant.

5 Place the dish in the oven and bake for about 30 minutes, until the sauce is bubbling and the cheese is golden brown. Remove from the oven and let cool for 10 minutes before serving with additional Marinara Sauce and fresh basil.

Salt, to taste

1 lb. elbow macaroni

7 tablespoons unsalted butter

2 cups panko

½ yellow onion, minced

3 tablespoons all-purpose flour

1 tablespoon yellow mustard

1 teaspoon turmeric

1 teaspoon garlic powder

1 teaspoon white pepper

2 cups light cream

2 cups whole milk

1 lb. American cheese, sliced

10 oz. Boursin cheese

½ lb. extra-sharp cheddar cheese, sliced

YIELD: 6 SERVINGS

ACTIVE TIME: 30 MINUTES

TOTAL TIME: 1 HOUR

MAC & CHEESE WITH BROWNED BUTTER BREAD CRUMBS

1   Preheat the oven to 400°F. Fill a Dutch oven with water and bring it to a boil. Add salt and the macaroni and cook until the macaroni is just shy of al dente, about 7 minutes. Drain and set aside.

2   Place the pot over medium heat and add 3 tablespoons of the butter. Cook until the butter starts to give off a nutty smell and brown. Add the bread crumbs, stir, and cook until the bread crumbs start to look like wet sand, about 4 minutes. Remove the bread crumbs from the pan and set it aside.

3   Wipe out the Dutch oven, place it over medium-high heat, and add the onion and the remaining butter. Cook, while stirring, until the onion is soft, about 10 minutes. Gradually add the flour, stirring constantly to prevent lumps from forming. Add the mustard, turmeric, garlic powder, and white pepper and stir until combined. Stir in the light cream and the milk, reduce the heat to medium, and bring the mixture to a simmer.

4   Add the cheeses one at a time, stirring to incorporate before adding the next one. When all of the cheeses have been incorporated and the mixture is smooth, cook until the flour taste is gone, about 10 minutes. Stir in the macaroni and top with the bread crumbs.

5   Place the Dutch oven in the oven and bake until the bread crumbs are crispy, 10 to 15 minutes. Remove from the oven and serve immediately.

YIELD: 4 SERVINGS

ACTIVE TIME: 10 MINUTES

TOTAL TIME: 45 MINUTES

CHICKEN CONGEE

4 cups Chicken Stock (see page 37)

2 tablespoons olive oil

1 garlic clove, minced

1½ cups long-grain rice

Salt and pepper, to taste

2 cups cooked and shredded chicken breast

1 teaspoon turmeric (optional)

Fresh cilantro, finely chopped, for garnish

1   Place the stock in a Dutch oven and bring to a simmer over medium heat.

2   Place the oil in a cast-iron wok or skillet and warm it over medium heat. When the oil starts to shimmer, add the garlic and cook until it is fragrant and golden brown, about 2 minutes. Add the rice, stir until coated with the oil, and cook until the rice is golden brown, about 4 minutes.

3   Add the rice and garlic to the stock and season with salt and pepper. Cook, while stirring occasionally, until the rice is tender, about 20 minutes.

4   Stir in the chicken and turmeric (if using) and cook until warmed through. Ladle into warmed bowls and garnish with cilantro.

FOR THE SESAME CHICKEN

2 tablespoons olive oil, plus ½ teaspoon

2-inch piece of fresh ginger, peeled and sliced

2 scallions, trimmed and minced

2 garlic cloves, minced

Juice of ½ lemon

4 boneless, skinless chicken breasts

Salt and pepper, to taste

3 tablespoons sesame seeds

FOR THE SHISHITO PEPPERS

3 tablespoons olive oil

1 lb. shishito peppers

Salt, to taste

YIELD: 4 SERVINGS

ACTIVE TIME: 20 MINUTES

TOTAL TIME: 1 HOUR

SESAME CHICKEN WITH BLISTERED SHISHITO PEPPERS

1   To begin preparations for the sesame chicken, place the 2 tablespoons of olive oil in a small skillet and warm over medium-high heat. When it starts shimmering, add the ginger, scallions, garlic, and lemon juice and sauté until the scallions are translucent, about 3 minutes. Remove the pan from heat and transfer the mixture to a small bowl.

2   Season the chicken breasts with pepper and salt and put them in a resealable plastic bag. Add the ginger-and-scallion mixture and press it around the chicken breasts. Seal and let it rest at room temperature for 30 minutes.

3   Preheat your gas or charcoal grill to medium-high heat (about 450°F). In a small dish, combine the remaining olive oil with the sesame seeds. Set the mixture aside.

4   Place the chicken on the grill and sprinkle the tops with half of the dressed sesame seeds. Grill the chicken breasts for about 7 minutes. Turn the chicken over, sprinkle the remaining sesame seeds on top, and grill the breasts until they feel springy when poked, 5 to 6 minutes. Transfer to a plate and tent with aluminum foil to keep them warm.

5   To prepare the shishito peppers, place the olive oil in a large cast-iron skillet and warm it over medium heat. When the oil starts to shimmer, add the peppers and cook, turning once or twice, until they are blistered and golden brown all over, about 2 minutes. Transfer to a paper towel–lined plate, season with salt, and serve alongside the chicken.

YIELD: 4 SERVINGS

ACTIVE TIME: 25 MINUTES

TOTAL TIME: 1 HOUR AND 30 MINUTES

CHIPOTLE CHICKEN ENCHILADAS

1 To prepare the sauce, bring water to a boil in a small saucepan. Add the chipotles and cook until they are reconstituted, about 10 minutes. Drain and transfer the chipotles to a food processor. Add the remaining ingredients and blitz until smooth. Add the puree to the skillet and cook over medium-low heat until the sauce is thick enough to coat the back of a spoon, about 15 to 20 minutes. Remove the sauce from the pan and set it aside.

2 To begin preparations for the enchiladas, place a large cast-iron skillet over medium-high heat and warm 2 tablespoons of the oil in it. Season the chicken with salt and pepper and add it to the pan. Sear the chicken on both sides and then add 1½ cups of the stock. Cover and cook until the chicken is tender enough to shred with a fork, about 20 minutes. Remove the chicken, transfer it to a mixing bowl, and shred with two forks.

3 Add the remaining oil and the potatoes to the skillet. Cook for 5 minutes, add the onion and garlic, and cook, stirring frequently, until the onion starts to soften, about 5 minutes.

4 Reduce the heat to medium and stir in the shredded chicken, the remaining stock, the green chilies, and 1 tablespoon of the sauce. Cook until the stock has evaporated, about 5 to 10 minutes. Remove the mixture from the pan and set it aside.

5 Preheat the oven to 375°F and oil a 9 x 13–inch baking pan with nonstick cooking spray. Place the tortillas on a work surface and spread a small amount of sauce on each of them. Divide the filling between the tortillas and roll them up. Place the tortillas, seam side down, in the baking pan.

6 Top the enchiladas with the remaining sauce and place the pan in the oven. Bake for 20 minutes, or until a crust forms on the exterior of the tortillas. Garnish with the Cotija cheese and cilantro and serve.

FOR THE SAUCE

4 dried chipotle chili peppers

½ (7 oz.) can of diced green chilies

2 tablespoons olive oil

3 plum tomatoes, seeded

1 tablespoon tomato paste

1 tablespoon cumin

1 teaspoon dried oregano

Salt and pepper, to taste

FOR THE ENCHILADAS

¼ cup olive oil

6 boneless, skinless chicken thighs

Salt and pepper, to taste

2 cups Chicken Stock (see page 37)

2 russet potatoes, peeled and minced

½ white onion, minced

2 garlic cloves, minced

½ (7 oz.) can of diced mild green chilies

24 Corn Tortillas (see page 77)

½ cup crumbled Cotija cheese, for garnish

Fresh cilantro, finely chopped, for garnish

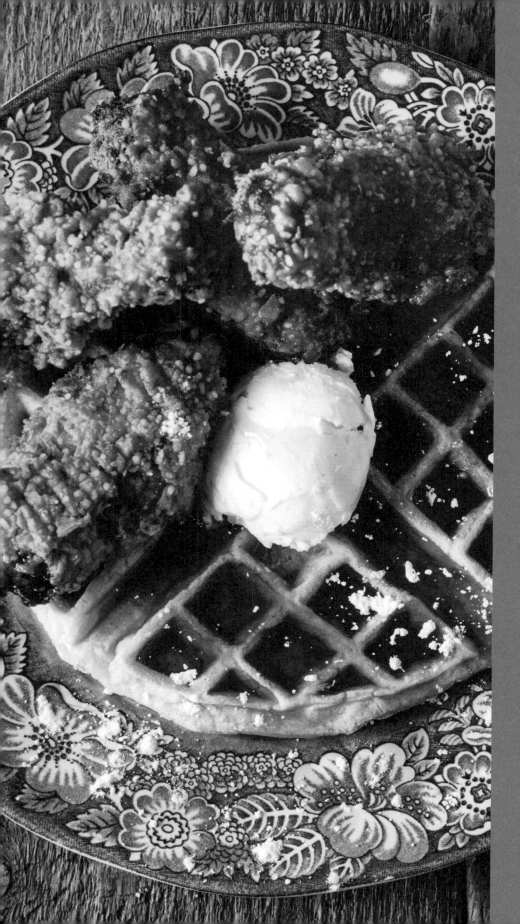

FOR THE CHICKEN

6 bone-in, skin-on chicken pieces

¼ cup all-purpose flour

Salt and pepper, to taste

1 cup milk

1 tablespoon white vinegar

2 eggs, lightly beaten

1½ cups cornflakes, finely crushed

½ cup bread crumbs

1 teaspoon paprika

6 tablespoons vegetable oil

FOR THE WAFFLES

2 tablespoons unsalted butter, melted, plus more as needed

2 cups all-purpose flour

4 teaspoons baking powder

½ teaspoon kosher salt

¼ cup sugar

2 eggs, whites and yolks separated

½ cup vegetable oil

2 cups whole milk

1 teaspoon pure vanilla extract

Maple syrup, for serving

YIELD: 6 SERVINGS

ACTIVE TIME: 45 MINUTES

TOTAL TIME: 1 HOUR AND 30 MINUTES

CHICKEN & WAFFLES

1 Preheat the oven to 400°F and place a cast-iron skillet in the oven as it warms. To begin preparations for the chicken, rinse the chicken pieces under cold water and pat them dry.

2 In a shallow bowl or cake pan, add the flour and salt and pepper and whisk to combine. Place the milk and vinegar in another bowl and let the mixture sit for 10 minutes. Stir the eggs into the milk mixture. In another large bowl, combine the cornflakes, bread crumbs, paprika, and 2 tablespoons of the vegetable oil.

3 Dip the chicken pieces into the seasoned flour, then the milk mixture, then the bread crumb mixture, until the pieces are completely coated. Put the pieces on a plate, cover with plastic wrap, and refrigerate for about 15 minutes.

4 Put on oven mitts, remove the skillet from the oven, and put the remaining oil in it. Heat it on low until the oil is 350°F. Place the cold chicken pieces in the skillet and turn in the hot oil until both sides are browned.

5 Put the skillet back in the oven and bake for about 30 minutes, turning the pieces over after 15 minutes. The chicken is done when the juices run clear when pierced with a fork. Remove from the oven, tent the skillet with aluminum foil, and begin preparations for the waffles.

6 Grease a waffle iron or skillet with the melted butter. Sift the dry ingredients together in a large mixing bowl. In a separate mixing bowl, add the egg yolks, oil, milk, and vanilla and stir until just combined. Add the wet mixture to the dry mixture and stir until thoroughly combined. Add the egg whites and fold to incorporate.

7 If using a waffle iron, add the batter and cook on medium-high heat for 5 to 10 minutes. If using a skillet, warm over medium heat until the butter starts to sizzle. Spoon about ½ cup of batter into the pan and let it spread into a circle. Lower the heat to medium-low and cook until the bottom of the waffle is set and bubbles begin to form on the top. Flip the waffle over and cook until set. Transfer to a wire rack and repeat until all of the batter has been used. To serve, top the waffles with the fried chicken and serve with maple syrup.

YIELD: 6 SERVINGS

ACTIVE TIME: 40 MINUTES

TOTAL TIME: 1 HOUR

SPAGHETTI & MEATBALLS

2 tablespoons olive oil

1 small onion, minced

3 garlic cloves, minced

¼ teaspoon red pepper flakes

1 large egg

2 tablespoons whole milk

½ cup Italian bread crumbs

¼ cup grated Parmesan cheese

¼ cup grated fresh mozzarella cheese

2 tablespoons finely chopped fresh parsley

1 teaspoon Italian seasoning

½ lb. ground pork

½ lb. ground beef

¼ lb. ground veal

Salt and pepper, to taste

1 lb. spaghetti

2 cups Marinara Sauce (see sidebar)

1 Preheat the broiler to high, position a rack so that the tops of the meatballs will be approximately 6 inches below the broiler, and line a rimmed baking sheet with aluminum foil.

2 Place the oil in a large skillet and warm over medium-high heat. When it starts to shimmer, add the onion, garlic, and red pepper flakes and sauté until the onion is translucent, about 3 minutes. Remove the pan from heat and set it aside.

3 Place the egg, milk, bread crumbs, Parmesan, mozzarella, parsley, and Italian seasoning in a mixing bowl and stir until combined. Add the pork, beef, veal, and the onion mixture, season with salt and pepper, and stir until thoroughly combined. Working with wet hands, form the mixture into 1½-inch meatballs, arrange them on the baking sheet, and spray the tops with cooking spray.

4 Place the meatballs in the oven and broil until browned all over, turning them as they cook. Remove the meatballs from the oven and set them aside.

5 While the meatballs are in the oven, bring water to a boil in a large saucepan. Add salt and the spaghetti and cook until the pasta is al dente, about 8 minutes.

MARINARA SAUCE

Place 4 lbs. chopped tomatoes, 1 sliced yellow onion, 15 crushed garlic cloves, 2 teaspoons finely chopped fresh thyme, 2 teaspoons finely chopped fresh oregano, 2 tablespoons olive oil, 1½ tablespoons kosher salt, and 1 teaspoon black pepper in a large saucepan and cook, stirring constantly, over medium heat until the tomatoes begin to collapse, about 10 minutes. Reduce the heat to low and cook, stirring occasionally, for about 1½ hours, or until the flavor is to your liking. Stir in 2 tablespoons finely chopped fresh basil and 1 tablespoon finely chopped fresh parsley and season the sauce to taste. The sauce will be chunky. If you prefer a smoother texture, transfer the sauce to a blender and puree before serving.

6 Place the sauce in the skillet and warm it over medium heat. Add the meatballs to the sauce, reduce the heat to low, cover the pan, and simmer, turning the meatballs occasionally, until they are cooked through, about 15 minutes.

7 Drain the pasta and divide it between the serving plates. Ladle the sauce and meatballs over the top and serve.

YIELD: 6 SERVINGS

ACTIVE TIME: 15 MINUTES

TOTAL TIME: 24 HOURS

CHICKEN & TOMATILLO CASSEROLE

FOR THE MARINADE

1 tomatillo, husked, rinsed, and halved

1 plum tomato, halved

2 garlic cloves, crushed

1 shallot, halved

1 poblano pepper, stemmed, seeds and ribs removed, and halved

¼ cup olive oil

1 tablespoon kosher salt

1 tablespoon cumin

FOR THE CASSEROLE

2 lbs. boneless, skinless chicken breasts, sliced thin

2 eggs, beaten

1 (14 oz.) can of fire-roasted tomatoes

Pinch of kosher salt

14 Corn Tortillas (see page 77)

1 cup salsa verde

¼ cup crumbled Cotija cheese

1 To prepare the marinade, place all of the ingredients in a blender and puree until smooth.

2 To begin preparations for the casserole, place the chicken breasts in a large baking pan or resealable plastic bag. Pour the marinade over the chicken and let it marinate in the refrigerator overnight.

3 Preheat the oven to 375°F. Place the chicken and marinade in a square 8-inch baking dish, place it in the oven, and roast until the center of the chicken reaches 165°F, about 30 minutes. Remove the dish from the oven, remove the chicken, transfer it to a mixing bowl, and shred it with a fork. Add the eggs, tomatoes, and salt to the bowl and stir to combine.

4 Place four of the tortillas in the baking dish. Add half of the chicken mixture, top with four more tortillas, and add the remaining chicken mixture. Top with remaining tortillas, cover with the salsa verde, and then place the dish in the oven. Bake for about 30 minutes, until the center is hot. Remove, sprinkle the cheese on top, and return to the oven. Bake until the cheese has melted, remove, and serve.

YIELD: 4 SERVINGS

ACTIVE TIME: 15 MINUTES

TOTAL TIME: 35 MINUTES

LAMB & PEAS CURRY

1 tablespoon olive oil

1 onion, chopped

2 garlic cloves, minced

1-inch piece of fresh ginger, peeled and grated

1 lb. ground lamb

1 tablespoon curry powder

½ cup chopped tomatoes

1 cup frozen peas

Salt, to taste

2 tablespoons plain yogurt

Cooked jasmine rice, for serving (optional)

Naan, for serving (optional)

1   Place the oil in a large skillet and warm it over medium-high heat. When the oil starts to shimmer, add the onion and sauté until it starts to brown, about 10 minutes.

2   Add the garlic and ginger, cook for another 2 minutes, and then add the lamb, using a fork to break it up as it browns. Cook the lamb until fully browned, about 8 minutes.

3   Stir in the curry powder, cook for 1 minute, add the tomatoes, and cook until they start to collapse, about 5 minutes. Add the frozen peas and stir until they are cooked through. Season with salt, stir in the yogurt, and serve over rice or with naan.

TARE SAUCE

Place ½ cup Chicken Stock (see page 37), ½ cup soy sauce, ½ cup mirin, ¼ cup sake, ½ cup brown sugar, 2 smashed garlic cloves, 1 tablespoon minced ginger, and 2 sliced scallions in a small saucepan and bring to a simmer over low heat. Simmer for 10 minutes, stirring once or twice, and remove from heat. Let cool and strain before using.

YIELD: 4 SERVINGS

ACTIVE TIME: 15 MINUTES

TOTAL TIME: 25 MINUTES

CHICKEN TSUKUNE

2 lbs. chicken thighs, ground

1 large egg, lightly beaten

1 cup panko

2 teaspoons miso paste

2 tablespoons sake

1½ tablespoons mirin

½ teaspoon black pepper

Tare Sauce (see sidebar)

2 scallions, trimmed and sliced, for garnish

Sesame seeds, for garnish

1   Place the ground chicken, egg, bread crumbs, miso, sake, mirin, and the pepper in a bowl and stir to combine. Cover the bowl and place it in the refrigerator while you make the sauce.

2   When the sauce has been prepared, remove the chicken mixture from the refrigerator and form it into balls or ovals.

3   Preheat a gas or charcoal grill for high heat (about 500°F).

4   Lightly coat the grates of the grill with nonstick cooking spray. Place the meatballs on the grill and cook until they start to brown, about 3 minutes. Turn the meatballs over and cook until they are completely cooked through, about 4 minutes. Remove from the grill and lightly baste the cooked meatballs with some of the Tare Sauce.

5   Garnish the meatballs with the scallions and sesame seeds and serve alongside the remaining Tare Sauce.

NOTE: For a different presentation, thread the meatballs on skewers before adding them on the grill.

YIELD: 4 SERVINGS

ACTIVE TIME: 15 MINUTES

TOTAL TIME: 1 HOUR

BULGOGI WITH MUSAENGCHAE

2 lbs. pork tenderloin, sliced thin

4 garlic cloves, minced

1-inch piece of fresh ginger, peeled and minced

½ cup gochujang (Korean chili paste)

2 tablespoons soy sauce

3 tablespoons sesame oil

Sesame seeds, for garnish

2 scallions, trimmed and chopped, for garnish

Musaengchae (see sidebar), for serving

1   Place all of the ingredients, except for the garnishes and Musaengchae, in a bowl and stir to combine. Place the bowl in the refrigerator and let the pork marinate for 30 minutes.

2   Warm a 12-inch cast-iron skillet over high heat for 5 minutes. When it is extremely hot, add the marinated pork and sear, turning the pork as it browns, until it is cooked through, about 5 minutes.

3   Garnish with the sesame seeds and scallions and serve with the Musaengchae.

MUSAENGCHAE

Place 3 cups shredded daikon radish, 1 teaspoon gochujang powder, 2 tablespoons rice vinegar, 1 tablespoon kosher salt, and 1 tablespoon sugar in a mixing bowl and stir to combine. Let marinate for at least 1 hour before serving.

YIELD: 6 SERVINGS

ACTIVE TIME: 30 MINUTES

TOTAL TIME: 2 HOURS AND 30 MINUTES

GOULASH

2 tablespoons olive oil

3 lbs. beef chuck, trimmed

3 yellow onions, chopped

2 carrots, peeled and chopped

2 bell peppers, stemmed, seeds and ribs removed, and chopped

1 teaspoon caraway seeds

¼ cup all-purpose flour

3 tablespoons sweet Hungarian paprika

3 tablespoons tomato paste

2 garlic cloves, minced

1 teaspoon sugar

Salt and pepper, to taste

2 cups Beef Stock (see page 205)

1 lb. wide egg noodles

1 cup sour cream

1. Place the oil in a Dutch oven and warm over medium heat. When the oil starts to shimmer, add the meat in batches and cook until it is browned all over, taking care not to crowd the pot. Remove the browned beef and set aside.

2. Reduce the heat to medium-low. Let the pot cool for 2 minutes and then add the onions, carrots, and peppers. Stir to coat with the pan drippings and sauté the vegetables until they are golden brown, about 10 minutes. Add the caraway seeds, stir to incorporate, and cook until the seeds are fragrant, about 1 minute.

3. Stir in the flour, paprika, tomato paste, garlic, sugar, salt, and pepper, add the stock, and use a wooden spoon to scrape up any browned bits from the bottom of the pan.

4. Bring the goulash to a boil, reduce the heat, and let it simmer until it thickens slightly, about 10 minutes. Return the meat to the Dutch oven, cover, and simmer over low heat until the meat is very tender, about 2 hours.

5. Approximately 20 minutes before the goulash will be done, bring water to a boil in a large pot. Add the egg noodles to the boiling water and cook until al dente. Drain and set aside.

6. To serve, stir the sour cream into the goulash and then ladle it over the cooked egg noodles.

YIELD: 4 SERVINGS

ACTIVE TIME: 30 MINUTES

TOTAL TIME: 1 HOUR

BIGOS

2 tablespoons olive oil

½ lb. kielbasa, diced

6½ tablespoons unsalted butter

2 large onions, diced

Salt and pepper, to taste

1½ lbs. green cabbage, cored and diced

¾ lb. wide egg noodles

1   Warm a large skillet over medium heat for 1 minute. Add the oil and raise heat to medium-high. When the oil starts shimmering, add the kielbasa and cook, stirring occasionally, until it starts to brown and crisp, about 5 minutes. Use a slotted spoon to transfer the kielbasa to a small bowl.

2   Add 3 tablespoons of the butter to the skillet. When it has melted and stopped foaming, add the onions and a couple pinches of salt and cook, stirring frequently, until the onions are soft, 8 to 10 minutes. Add another 3 tablespoons of the butter, the cabbage, a few more pinches of salt, and a few pinches of pepper and stir to combine. When the mixture starts sizzling, cover the pan and reduce the heat to medium-low. Cook, stirring occasionally, until very soft and brown, 12 to 15 minutes.

3   As the onions and cabbage cook, bring a large pot of water to a boil. When it's boiling, add salt and stir until it has dissolved. Add the egg noodles and stir for the first minute to prevent any sticking. Cook until just shy of al dente, about 6 minutes. Reserve ¼ cup of the water and drain the noodles.

4   Return the pot to the stove. Immediately turn the heat to high and add the remaining butter and the reserved water. Add the drained noodles and toss to combine. Once the water has been absorbed by the noodles, add the kielbasa and onion-and-cabbage mixture and toss to evenly distribute. Cook for 1 to 2 minutes, gently stirring so as to not tear the noodles. Season to taste and serve immediately.

YIELD: 6 SERVINGS

ACTIVE TIME: 30 MINUTES

TOTAL TIME: 24 HOURS

CHILI CON CARNE

1½ lbs. ground beef

1 (28 oz.) can of crushed San Marzano tomatoes

1 red bell pepper, stemmed, seeds and ribs removed, and chopped

2 small yellow onions, chopped, plus more for garnish

4 garlic cloves, minced

1 jalapeño pepper, stemmed, seeds and ribs removed, and minced

1 lb. pinto beans, soaked overnight and drained

¼ cup finely chopped fresh cilantro, plus more for garnish

¼ cup hot sauce

2 tablespoons chili powder

1 tablespoon black pepper

1 tablespoon kosher salt

2 tablespoons garlic powder

⅓ cup cumin

1 tablespoon Madras curry powder

1 tablespoon dried oregano

Cheddar cheese, grated, for garnish

1   Place the ground beef in a Dutch oven and cook over medium heat, breaking it up with a fork as it browns, until it is cooked through, about 8 minutes.

2   Drain the fat from the beef, add all of the remaining ingredients, except for the garnishes, and stir to combine. Bring to a boil, reduce heat so that the chili gently simmers, and cook until the beans are fork-tender and the flavor is to your liking, 3 to 4 hours.

3   Ladle into warmed bowls and garnish with the cheddar cheese and the additional onion and cilantro.

YIELD: 6 SERVINGS

ACTIVE TIME: 15 MINUTES

TOTAL TIME: 4 HOURS

SPICY SAUSAGE & PEPPERS

5 bell peppers, stemmed, seeds and ribs removed, and sliced

1 (28 oz.) can of fire-roasted tomatoes

3 garlic cloves

2 chipotle peppers in adobo

1 tablespoon adobo sauce

2 lbs. kielbasa, cut into 6 pieces

1 habanero pepper, pierced

Submarine rolls, for serving (optional)

1   Place the bell peppers in a slow cooker and set it to high heat. Place the tomatoes, garlic, chipotles in adobo, and adobo sauce in a food processor and blitz until smooth. Pour the puree over the peppers and stir to combine.

2   Add the kielbasa and the habanero to the slow cooker, cover, and cook on high for 4 hours.

3   Remove the habanero and discard. Ladle the sausage and peppers into warmed bowls or submarine rolls and serve immediately.

YIELD: 6 SERVINGS

ACTIVE TIME: 10 MINUTES

TOTAL TIME: 1 HOUR

SKILLET MEATLOAF WITH BACON

1½ lbs. ground beef

½ lb. ground pork

1 yellow onion, minced

2 teaspoons garlic powder

1 cup bread crumbs

¼ cup whole milk

2 eggs, lightly beaten

2 tablespoons tomato paste

2 tablespoons Worcestershire sauce

2 teaspoons olive oil

8 strips of bacon

1   Preheat the oven to 375°F. Place the beef, pork, onion, garlic powder, bread crumbs, milk, eggs, tomato paste, and Worcestershire sauce in a bowl and work the mixture with your hands until thoroughly combined.

2   Coat a cast-iron skillet with the olive oil. Place the meat mixture in the pan and form it into a rectangle. Lay four slices of the bacon lengthwise over the top and place the remaining four on top crosswise, weaving them together.

3   Place the skillet in the oven and bake until the meatloaf is cooked through, about 45 minutes. Remove the meatloaf from the oven and let it cool for 10 minutes before slicing and serving.

YIELD: 4 SERVINGS   **ACTIVE TIME:** 20 MINUTES   **TOTAL TIME:** 45 MINUTES

LAMB & SWEET POTATO HASH

1 lb. sweet potatoes, peeled and minced

2 tablespoons unsalted butter, clarified

2 poblano peppers, stemmed, seeds and ribs removed, and chopped

2 yellow onions, minced

2 garlic cloves, minced

1 tablespoon cumin

3 cups chopped leftover lamb

1 tablespoon kosher salt, plus more to taste

1 tablespoon finely chopped fresh oregano

Black pepper, to taste

1   Fill a 12-inch cast-iron skillet with water and bring it to a boil. Add the sweet potatoes and cook until they are just tender, about 7 minutes. Be careful not to overcook them, as you don't want to end up with mashed potatoes. Drain the potatoes and set aside.

2   Add the clarified butter, poblano peppers, onions, garlic, and cumin to the skillet and sauté over medium heat until all of the vegetables are soft, about 10 minutes.

3   Add the lamb and return the potatoes to the skillet. Add the salt and cook until everything is warmed through, another 5 minutes. Stir in the oregano, season with pepper, and serve.

GOOD
COMPANY

If you had the ability to tailor the world to match your desires, you would only entertain your family and friends on those days where you had enough time to spend all day in the kitchen, ensuring that the prep was squared away by the time the company arrived, and that something delicious and unique lay in wait.

Things being what they are, that is rarely the case. The structure of the modern world means that most people's weekends are devoted to catching up on rest, errands, and hobbies, leaving little time for getting together and taking the time to enjoy good food and conversation. If you want to break bread with those you love, you've got to do so on a weekday, a thought that is anathema to most.

Until now. We've gathered a selection of dishes that one can confidently put forth any night of the week, no matter who happens by. All unique enough to transform an evening into an occasion, and simple enough that they appear much more demanding than they are in reality.

YIELD: 6 SERVINGS

ACTIVE TIME: 20 MINUTES

TOTAL TIME: 1 HOUR AND 30 MINUTES

MAPLE & MUSTARD PORK TENDERLOIN

2 lbs. red potatoes, cut into wedges

2 yellow onions, sliced

4 celery stalks, chopped

½ lb. carrots, washed and halved lengthwise

3 tablespoons olive oil

Salt and pepper, to taste

2½-lb. pork tenderloin

¼ cup real maple syrup

5 garlic cloves, minced

1 cup Chicken Stock (see page 37)

3 bay leaves

1   Preheat the oven to 375°F degrees. Place the potatoes, onions, celery, and carrots in a 9 x 13–inch baking pan. Add 2 tablespoons of the olive oil, season with salt and pepper, and toss to coat. Cover the pan with aluminum foil, place it in the oven, and roast for 30 minutes.

2   While the vegetables are roasting, rub the tenderloin with the maple syrup and the remaining olive oil. Season with salt and pepper and let the pork come to room temperature.

3   Remove the pan from the oven, remove the foil, and set it aside. Add the garlic, stock, and bay leaves to the pan. Place the tenderloin on top of the vegetables and return the pan to the oven. Roast for 45 to 50 minutes, or until the center of the tenderloin reaches 145°F.

4   Remove the pan from the oven and transfer the pork to a cutting board. Place the reserved foil over it and let the pork rest for 10 minutes.

5   Remove the carrots, celery, 1 cup of the onions, and the juices from the pan. Transfer to a food processor and blitz until smooth.

6   Slice the tenderloin into 1-inch-thick pieces. Place the potatoes and remaining onions on the serving plates, top with the pork, and drizzle the sauce over everything.

YIELD: 4 SERVINGS

ACTIVE TIME: 10 MINUTES

TOTAL TIME: 1 HOUR

TEA-SMOKED SALMON

½ cup olive oil, plus more as needed

½ cup mirin

1 tablespoon brown sugar

1-inch piece of fresh ginger

1 teaspoon orange zest

1½ lbs. skinless, center-cut salmon fillets

1 cup white rice

½ cup granulated sugar

1 cup green tea (gunpowder preferred)

1 orange peel, diced

1 In a mixing bowl, whisk together the oil, mirin, brown sugar, ginger, and orange zest. Add the salmon and let it marinate for 30 minutes.

2 Line a large wok with aluminum foil, making sure the foil extends over the sides of the wok. Add the rice, granulated sugar, tea, and orange peel to the wok and cook over high heat until the rice begins to smoke.

3 Place the salmon on a lightly oiled rack, set it above the smoking rice, and place the lid on top of the wok. Fold the foil over the lid to seal the wok as best as you can. Reduce the heat to medium and cook for 10 minutes.

4 Remove from heat and let the wok cool completely, about 20 minutes. When the wok is completely cool, the fish will be cooked to medium.

YIELD: 6 SERVINGS

ACTIVE TIME: 30 MINUTES

TOTAL TIME: 1 HOUR AND 20 MINUTES

CHICKEN LEGS WITH POTATOES & FENNEL

⅓ cup olive oil, plus 2 tablespoons

6 skin-on chicken legs

1 tablespoon kosher salt, plus more to taste

1 tablespoon black pepper, plus more to taste

5 shallots, diced

3 garlic cloves, minced

2 red potatoes, diced

4 Yukon Gold potatoes, diced

3 fennel bulbs, diced, fronds reserved for garnish

1 teaspoon celery seeds

1 teaspoon fennel seeds

½ cup sun-dried tomatoes in olive oil, drained

1 cup Chardonnay

6 tablespoons unsalted butter

1   Place a Dutch oven over medium-high heat and add the ⅓ cup of olive oil. Rub the chicken legs with the remaining oil and season them with the salt and pepper. When the oil starts to shimmer, add half of the chicken legs to the pot and cook until the skin is golden brown and crusted, about 5 minutes. Remove, set aside, and repeat with the remaining chicken legs.

2   Preheat the oven to 400°F. Add the shallots and garlic to the Dutch oven and use a wooden spoon to scrape all of the browned bits from the bottom. Sauté until the shallots are translucent, about 3 minutes. Raise the heat to high and add the remaining ingredients, except for the wine and the butter. Cook, stirring occasionally, for about 15 minutes.

3   Stir in the wine and the butter and then return the chicken to the pan, skin side up. Reduce the heat, cover, and cook until the potatoes are tender and the chicken is 155°F in the center, about 30 minutes. Remove the lid, transfer the Dutch oven to the oven, and cook until the chicken is 165°F in the center. Garnish with the fennel fronds and serve.

YIELD: 4 SERVINGS

ACTIVE TIME: 25 MINUTES

TOTAL TIME: 45 MINUTES

MASHED POTATO, BACON & SCALLION PIZZA

1 ball of pizza dough (see page 94 for homemade), stretched into a 10-inch round

2 tablespoons olive oil

Salt and pepper, to taste

2 tablespoons grated Asiago cheese

¾ cup mashed potatoes

1½ cups grated mozzarella cheese

Heavy cream, to taste

4 strips of bacon, cooked and chopped

½ cup chopped scallions

1 teaspoon finely chopped fresh parsley

1 teaspoon finely chopped fresh rosemary

1 teaspoon finely chopped fresh thyme

1   Preheat the oven to 550°F. Brush the dough with olive oil. Season it with pepper and sprinkle the Asiago over the dough. Spread the mashed potatoes over the dough and then top with the mozzarella.

2   Drizzle the pizza generously with the cream and top with the bacon, scallions, and fresh herbs. Season the pizza with salt and place it in the oven. Cook, while rotating the pizza halfway through, until golden brown, about 15 to 20 minutes. Remove from the oven and let cool slightly before serving.

5 tablespoons green curry paste

6 boneless, skinless chicken thighs

2 yellow onions, sliced

2 red bell peppers, stemmed, seeds and ribs removed, and sliced

3-inch piece of fresh ginger, peeled and mashed

1 garlic clove, mashed

3 tablespoons fish sauce

1 tablespoon Madras curry powder

1 (14 oz.) can of coconut milk

2 tablespoons finely chopped fresh Thai basil, plus more for garnish

1½ cups basmati rice

1 cup water

Fresh cilantro, finely chopped, for garnish

Lime wedges, for serving

YIELD: 4 SERVINGS

ACTIVE TIME: 25 MINUTES

TOTAL TIME: 1 HOUR AND 30 MINUTES

COCONUT CURRY CHICKEN WITH BASMATI RICE

1   Preheat the oven to 375°F. Rub 2 tablespoons of the green curry paste on the chicken and let it rest at room temperature for 30 minutes.

2   Place a large cast-iron skillet over medium-high heat and add the chicken. Cook until browned, turn over, and cook for another 3 minutes. Remove the chicken from the skillet and set it aside.

3   Add the onions, peppers, ginger, and garlic to the pan and cook, stirring frequently and scraping the pan to remove any browned bits from the bottom, for 5 to 7 minutes.

4   When the vegetables are tender, add the remaining green curry paste and cook for an additional 3 minutes, until fragrant.

5   Add the fish sauce, Madras curry powder, coconut milk, and Thai basil and stir until combined. Add the rice and water, stir, and then return the chicken to the pan. Cover the skillet and place it in the oven. Bake until the rice is tender and has absorbed all of the liquid, about 25 minutes. Garnish with the cilantro and additional Thai basil and serve with the lime wedges.

YIELD: 4 SERVINGS

ACTIVE TIME: 20 MINUTES

TOTAL TIME: 20 MINUTES

TERIYAKI SALMON WITH VEGETABLES

FOR THE TERIYAKI SAUCE

1-inch piece of fresh ginger, peeled and minced

3 garlic cloves, minced

1 tablespoon rice vinegar

2 tablespoons brown sugar

¼ cup soy sauce

1 tablespoon cornstarch

½ cup water

FOR THE SALMON & VEGETABLES

3 tablespoons olive oil

4 Chinese eggplants, sliced

1 red bell pepper, stemmed, seeds and ribs removed, and sliced thin

2 tablespoons chopped scallions

1 cup bean sprouts

1½ lbs. salmon fillets

Salt and pepper, to taste

1 To prepare the teriyaki sauce, place all of the ingredients in a food processor and blitz until smooth. Place it in a saucepan and cook, while stirring, over medium heat until the sauce starts to thicken, about 6 minutes. Place the sauce in a bowl and set it aside.

2 Preheat the oven to 375°F. To begin preparations for the salmon and vegetables, place the olive oil in a large cast-iron skillet and warm it over medium-high heat. When the oil starts to shimmer, add the eggplants, bell pepper, and scallions to the pan and sauté until the eggplants start to collapse, about 5 minutes. Add the bean sprouts and stir to incorporate.

3 Place the salmon on top of the vegetables, skin side down, season with salt, pepper, and some of the teriyaki sauce and transfer the pan to the oven. Bake until the salmon is cooked through, about 8 minutes, remove the pan from the oven, top with more of the teriyaki sauce, and serve.

YIELD: 4 SERVINGS

ACTIVE TIME: 15 MINUTES

TOTAL TIME: 25 MINUTES

SPRING PEA SOUP WITH LEMON RICOTTA

1 cup ricotta cheese

¼ cup heavy cream

2 tablespoons lemon zest

1 tablespoon kosher salt, plus 2 teaspoons

12 cups water

6 strips of lemon peel

3 cups fresh peas

3 shallots, diced

6 fresh mint leaves, plus more for garnish

1   Place the ricotta, cream, lemon zest, and the 2 teaspoons of salt in a food processor and blitz until smooth. Season to taste and set aside.

2   Place the water and remaining salt in a saucepan and bring to a boil over medium heat. Add the strips of lemon peel to the saucepan along with the peas and shallots. Cook for 2 to 3 minutes, until the peas are just cooked through. Drain, making sure to reserve 2 cups of the cooking liquid, and immediately transfer the peas, strips of lemon peel, and shallots to a blender. Add the mint leaves and half of the reserved cooking liquid, and puree until the desired consistency is achieved, adding more cooking liquid as needed.

3   Season to taste, ladle into warmed bowls, and place a spoonful of the lemon ricotta in each portion. Garnish with additional mint and serve immediately, as the brilliant green color starts to fade as the soup cools.

THAI RED DUCK CURRY

4 skin-on duck breasts

¼ cup Thai red curry paste

2½ cups coconut milk

10 makrut lime leaves (optional)

1 cup diced pineapple

1 tablespoon fish sauce, plus more to taste

1 tablespoon brown sugar

6 bird's eye chili peppers, stemmed, seeds and ribs removed, and sliced

20 cherry tomatoes

1 cup fresh basil (Thai basil strongly recommended)

1½ cups cooked jasmine rice, for serving

1 Use a very sharp knife to slash the skin on the duck breasts, taking care not to cut all the way through to the meat.

2 Place a Dutch oven over medium-high heat. Place the duck breasts, skin side down, in the pot and sear until browned, about 4 minutes. This will render a lot of the fat.

3 Turn the duck breasts over and cook until browned on the other side, about 4 minutes. Remove the duck from the pot, let it cool, drain most of the rendered duck fat, and reserve it for another preparation.

4 When the duck breasts are cool enough to handle, remove the skin and discard it. Cut each breast into 2-inch pieces.

5 Set the heat to medium, add the curry paste to the Dutch oven, and sauté for 2 minutes. Add the coconut milk, bring to a boil, and cook for 5 minutes.

6 Reduce the heat, return the duck to the pot, and simmer for 8 minutes. Add the lime leaves (if using), pineapple, fish sauce, brown sugar, and chilies, stir to incorporate, and simmer for 5 minutes. Skim to remove any fat from the top as the curry simmers. Taste and add more fish sauce if necessary. Stir in the cherry tomatoes and basil and serve over the jasmine rice.

YIELD: 4 SERVINGS

ACTIVE TIME: 20 MINUTES

TOTAL TIME: 1 HOUR AND 30 MINUTES

ROGAN JOSH

3 tablespoons olive oil

2 lbs. boneless lamb shoulder, cut into 1-inch pieces

Salt, to taste

2 large yellow onions, sliced thin

2-inch piece of fresh ginger, peeled and minced

2 garlic cloves, minced

1 tablespoon curry powder, plus 1 teaspoon

1 teaspoon turmeric

1 teaspoon cayenne pepper, or to taste

1 teaspoon garam masala

1 (14 oz.) can of crushed tomatoes

1 cup plain yogurt

2 cups water

Fresh cilantro, finely chopped, for garnish

Red onion, minced, for garnish

1   Place the oil in a Dutch oven and warm it over medium-high heat. Generously season the lamb with salt. When the oil starts to shimmer, add the lamb and cook, turning occasionally, until it is lightly browned all over, about 10 minutes. Remove the lamb with a slotted spoon and set it aside.

2   Add the yellow onions, ginger, garlic, curry powder, turmeric, cayenne, and garam masala to the Dutch oven and sauté for 2 minutes. Add the tomatoes, yogurt, and water and bring to a gentle boil. Return the lamb to the pot, reduce the heat, cover, and simmer until the lamb is very tender, about 1 hour, stirring occasionally.

3   Ladle into warmed bowls and garnish with the cilantro and red onion.

YIELD: 6 SERVINGS

ACTIVE TIME: 1 HOUR

TOTAL TIME: 2 HOURS AND 30 MINUTES

FRENCH ONION SOUP

3 tablespoons unsalted butter

7 large sweet onions, sliced

2 teaspoons kosher salt

⅓ cup orange juice

3 oz. sherry

3 tablespoons finely chopped fresh thyme

7 cups Beef Stock (see page 205)

3 garlic cloves, minced

2 teaspoons black pepper

6 slices of day-old bread

1 cup shredded Gruyère cheese

1 cup shredded Emmental cheese

1 Place the butter, onions, and salt in a Dutch oven and cook over low heat, stirring frequently. Cook until the onions are dark brown and caramelized, 40 minutes to 1 hour.

2 Deglaze the pot with the orange juice and sherry, using a wooden spoon to scrape any browned bits from the bottom of the pot. Add the thyme, stock, and garlic, raise the heat to medium, and bring to a simmer. Simmer for 1 hour.

3 While the soup is simmering, preheat the oven to 450°F.

4 After 1 hour, ladle the soup into oven-safe bowls and place a slice of bread on top of each portion. Sprinkle the cheeses over each bowl, place them in the oven, and bake until the cheese begins to brown, about 10 minutes. Carefully remove the bowls from the oven and let cool for 10 minutes before serving.

YIELD: 4 SERVINGS

ACTIVE TIME: 20 MINUTES

TOTAL TIME: I HOUR AND 45 MINUTES

SWEET & SPICY ROASTED BARLEY

5 carrots, peeled and chopped

Olive oil, as needed

Salt and pepper, to taste

6 dried pasilla peppers

2¼ cups boiling water

1 cup pearl barley

1 red onion, minced

2 tablespoons adobo seasoning

1 tablespoon sugar

1 tablespoon chili powder

¼ cup finely chopped fresh oregano

1 Preheat the oven to 375°F. Place the carrots in a 9 x 13-inch baking pan, drizzle olive oil over them, and season with salt and pepper. Place the pan in the oven and roast the carrots until they are soft to the touch, about 45 minutes.

2 While the carrots are roasting, open the pasilla peppers and discard the seeds and stems. Place the peppers in a bowl, add the boiling water, and cover the bowl with aluminum foil.

3 When the carrots are cooked, remove the pan from the oven and add the remaining ingredients and the liquid the peppers have been soaking in. Chop the reconstituted peppers, add them to the pan, and spread the mixture so that the liquid is covering the barley. Cover the pan tightly with aluminum foil, place it in the oven, and bake until the barley is tender, about 45 minutes. Fluff with a fork and serve immediately.

YIELD: 4 SERVINGS

ACTIVE TIME: 10 MINUTES

TOTAL TIME: 2 DAYS

GREEN BEAN & TOFU CASSEROLE

FOR THE MARINADE

3 tablespoons soy sauce

2 tablespoons rice vinegar

1 tablespoon sesame oil

1 tablespoon honey

Pinch of cinnamon

Pinch of black pepper

FOR THE CASSEROLE

1 lb. extra-firm tofu, drained and chopped

1 lb. green beans

4 oz. shiitake mushrooms, sliced

2 tablespoons sesame oil

1 tablespoon soy sauce

2 tablespoons sesame seeds, for garnish

1 To prepare the marinade, place all of the ingredients in a small bowl and stir to combine.

2 To begin preparations for the casserole, place the marinade and the tofu in a resealable plastic bag, place it in the refrigerator, and let it marinate for 2 days, gently shaking the bag occasionally.

3 Preheat the oven to 375°F. Remove the cubes of tofu from the bag. Place the green beans, mushrooms, sesame oil, and soy sauce in the bag and shake until the vegetables are coated.

4 Line a 9 x 13–inch baking pan with parchment paper and place the tofu on it in an even layer. Place in the oven and roast for 35 minutes. Remove the pan, flip the cubes of tofu over, and push them to the edge of the pan. Add the green bean-and-mushroom mixture, return the pan to the oven, and roast for 15 minutes, or until the green beans are cooked to your preference. Remove the pan from the oven, garnish with the sesame seeds, and serve.

YIELD: 4 SERVINGS

ACTIVE TIME: 30 MINUTES

TOTAL TIME: 3 HOURS

CARNE ASADA

1 jalapeño pepper, stemmed, seeds and ribs removed, and minced

3 garlic cloves, minced

½ cup finely chopped fresh cilantro

¼ cup olive oil, plus more as needed

Juice of 1 small orange

2 tablespoons apple cider vinegar

2 teaspoons cayenne pepper

1 teaspoon ancho chili powder

1 teaspoon garlic powder

1 teaspoon paprika

1 teaspoon kosher salt

1 teaspoon cumin

1 teaspoon dried oregano

¼ teaspoon black pepper

2 lbs. flank or skirt steak, trimmed

Corn Tortillas (see page 77), for serving

1 Place all of the ingredients, except for the steak and the tortillas, in a baking dish or a large resealable plastic bag and stir to combine. Add the steak, place it in the refrigerator, and let marinate for at least 2 hours. If time allows, marinate the steak overnight.

2 Approximately 30 minutes before you are going to cook the steak, remove it from the marinade, pat it dry, and let it come to room temperature.

3 Place a large cast-iron skillet over high heat and add enough oil to coat the bottom. When the oil starts to shimmer, add the steak and cook on each side for 4 minutes for medium-rare.

4 Remove the steak from the pan and let rest for 5 minutes before slicing it into thin strips, making sure to cut against the grain. Serve with the tortillas and your favorite taco fixings.

YIELD: 4 SERVINGS

ACTIVE TIME: 10 MINUTES

TOTAL TIME: 1 HOUR AND 30 MINUTES

SICHUAN CUMIN BEEF

3 tablespoons cumin seeds

2 teaspoons Sichuan peppercorns

1 teaspoon kosher salt

3 tablespoons olive oil

4 dried red chili peppers, chopped

2 teaspoons red pepper flakes

1½ lbs. beef chuck, cut into 1-inch pieces

1 yellow onion, sliced

2 scallions, trimmed and sliced thin, for garnish

½ cup finely chopped fresh cilantro, for garnish

1   Place the cumin seeds and Sichuan peppercorns in a dry skillet and toast over medium heat until they are fragrant, about 1 minute, making sure they do not burn. Remove and grind the mixture into a fine powder with a mortar and pestle.

2   Place the salt, 2 tablespoons of the oil, the dried chilies, red pepper flakes, and the toasted spice powder in a large bowl and stir to combine. Add the beef and toss until coated. Cover the bowl with a kitchen towel and let it stand for 1 hour.

3   Warm a cast-iron skillet over high heat until the pan is extremely hot. Add the remaining oil, swirl to coat, and then add the beef and onion. Cook, stirring occasionally, until the beef is browned all over and cooked through, about 10 minutes. Garnish with the scallions and cilantro and serve immediately.

TIP: Lamb or chicken will also work well in this preparation.

YIELD: 4 SERVINGS

ACTIVE TIME: 15 MINUTES

TOTAL TIME: 35 MINUTES

PAD THAI

6 oz. wide rice noodles

1 tablespoon olive oil

3 boneless, skinless chicken breasts

1 large egg

¼ cup tamarind paste

2 tablespoons water

1½ tablespoons fish sauce

2 tablespoons rice vinegar

1½ tablespoons brown sugar

4 scallions, trimmed and sliced

1 cup bean sprouts

½ teaspoon cayenne pepper

¼ cup crushed peanuts

Lime wedges, for serving

1   Place the noodles in a baking dish and cover them with boiling water. Stir and let stand until they are tender, about 15 minutes.

2   Place the oil in a large wok or skillet and warm it over medium-high heat. When the oil starts to shimmer, add the chicken and cook until it is browned on both sides and springy to the touch, about 8 minutes. Remove the chicken from the pan and let it cool briefly. When cool enough to handle, slice the chicken into thin strips.

3   Add the noodles and the egg and cook until the egg is set. While stirring to incorporate with every addition, add the tamarind paste, water, fish sauce, vinegar, brown sugar, scallions, bean sprouts, cayenne pepper, and peanuts. Return the chicken to the pan, cook until everything is warmed through, and then serve with the lime wedges.

YIELD: 4 SERVINGS

ACTIVE TIME: 30 MINUTES

TOTAL TIME: I HOUR

LOBSTER TOSTADAS WITH CORN SALSA & CILANTRO-LIME SOUR CREAM

1   Preheat your gas or charcoal grill to medium heat (about 400°F). To begin preparations for the tostadas and salsa, drizzle olive oil over the corn and season it with salt and pepper. Place the corn on the grill and cook, while turning, until charred all over, about 8 minutes. Remove from the grill and let cool.

2   When the corn is cool enough to handle, remove the kernels and place them in a mixing bowl. Add the jalapeño, onion, garlic, lime juice, cilantro, and tomato and stir to combine. Set the salsa aside.

3   To prepare the sour cream, place all of the ingredients in a mixing bowl, stir to combine, and set aside.

4   Place the canola oil in a Dutch oven and warm to 350°F over medium-high heat. Working with one tortilla at a time, place them into the oil and fry until crispy and golden brown. Remove from the oil, transfer to a paper towel–lined plate, and season with salt and paprika.

5   Spread some sour cream on each tortilla and top with the salsa and lobster meat. Garnish with jalapeño, cilantro, and red cabbage and serve with lime wedges.

FOR THE TOSTADAS & SALSA

1 tablespoon olive oil

2 ears of corn, husked

Salt and pepper, to taste

1 small jalapeño pepper, stemmed, seeds and ribs removed, and diced, plus more for garnish

¼ red onion, chopped

1 garlic clove, minced

1½ tablespoons fresh lime juice

¼ cup finely chopped fresh cilantro, plus more for garnish

½ cup diced tomato

2 cups canola oil

8 Corn Tortillas (see page 77)

Paprika, to taste

Meat from 4 cooked chicken lobsters

Red cabbage, diced, for garnish

Lime wedges, for serving

FOR THE SOUR CREAM

½ cup finely chopped fresh cilantro

¼ cup fresh lime juice

1¼ cups sour cream

1½ teaspoons kosher salt

½ teaspoon black pepper

1 stick of unsalted butter

2 yellow onions, chopped

1 small butternut squash, peeled and chopped

1 tablespoon kosher salt, plus 2 teaspoons

3 cups whole milk

5 cups Vegetable Stock (see page 22)

2 cups Arborio rice

2 cups white wine

3 cups baby kale, stemmed and chopped

¾ cup toasted walnuts

½ cup dried cranberries

Fresh lemon juice, to taste

YIELD: 6 SERVINGS

ACTIVE TIME: 35 MINUTES

TOTAL TIME: I HOUR AND 20 MINUTES

SQUASH RISOTTO WITH BABY KALE, TOASTED WALNUTS & DRIED CRANBERRIES

1. Place 2 tablespoons of the butter in a saucepan and melt it over medium heat. Add one of the onions and cook until it is translucent, about 3 minutes. Add the squash, the tablespoon of salt, and the milk, reduce the heat to low, and cook until the squash is tender, about 20 minutes. Strain, discard the cooking liquid, and transfer the squash and onion to a blender. Puree until smooth and then set aside.

2. Place the stock in a saucepan, bring to a boil, and remove from heat.

3. Place the remaining butter in a large skillet with high sides and melt over medium heat. Add the remaining onion and sauté until translucent, about 3 minutes. Add the rice and remaining salt and cook, stirring constantly, until you can smell a toasted nutty aroma. Be careful not to brown the rice.

4. Deglaze the pan with the white wine and continue to stir until all the liquid has been absorbed. Add the stock in 1-cup increments and stir constantly until all of the stock has been absorbed by the rice.

5. Add the squash puree and kale, stir to incorporate, and season to taste. Stir in the walnuts, dried cranberries, and lemon juice, and serve immediately.

YIELD: 6 SERVINGS

ACTIVE TIME: 45 MINUTES

TOTAL TIME: 2 HOURS

CHICKEN BOLOGNESE WITH PENNE

2 tablespoons olive oil

½ lb. bacon

1½ lbs. ground chicken

Salt and pepper, to taste

1 onion, chopped

1 carrot, peeled and minced

3 celery stalks, chopped

2 garlic cloves, minced

1 tablespoon finely chopped fresh thyme

2 cups sherry

8 cups Marinara Sauce (see page 115)

1 cup water

1 cup heavy cream

2 tablespoons finely chopped fresh sage

1 lb. penne

4 tablespoons unsalted butter

1 cup grated Parmesan cheese, plus more for garnish

1 tablespoon finely chopped fresh basil, for garnish

Red pepper flakes, for garnish (optional)

1   Place the olive oil and bacon in a Dutch oven and cook over medium heat until the bacon is crispy, about 6 minutes. Add the chicken, season with salt and pepper, and cook, breaking the chicken up with a fork as it browns, until it is cooked through, about 8 minutes. Remove the bacon and the chicken from the pot and set them aside.

2   Add the onion, carrot, celery, and garlic to the Dutch oven, season with salt, and sauté until the carrot is tender, about 8 minutes. Return the bacon and chicken to the pan, add the thyme and sherry, and cook until the sherry has nearly evaporated. Add the Marinara Sauce and water, reduce the heat to low, and cook for approximately 45 minutes, stirring often, until the sauce has thickened to the desired consistency.

3   Stir the cream and sage into the sauce and cook for an additional 15 minutes.

4   Bring a large pot of water to a boil. Add salt and the penne and cook until it is just shy of al dente, about 6 minutes. Reserve 1 cup of the pasta water, drain the penne, and then return it to the pot. Add the butter, bolognese, and reserved pasta water and stir to combine. Add the Parmesan and stir until melted. Garnish with additional Parmesan, the basil, and red pepper flakes, if desired.

FOR THE MARINADE

2 tablespoons rice vinegar

3 tablespoons soy sauce

1 tablespoon toasted
sesame oil

½ teaspoon sugar

2 garlic cloves, minced

FOR THE DRESSING

1 tablespoon rice vinegar

1 tablespoon peanut oil

1 teaspoon soy sauce

1 tablespoon toasted
sesame oil

1-inch piece of fresh ginger,
peeled and grated

FOR THE NOODLES

3 eggplants (about 2 lbs.)

½ lb. soba noodles

3 tablespoons peanut oil

Salt, to taste

¾ lb. extra-firm tofu,
drained and diced

6 scallions, trimmed
and chopped

YIELD: 4 SERVINGS

ACTIVE TIME: 45 MINUTES

TOTAL TIME: I HOUR AND 45 MINUTES

SOBA NOODLES WITH MARINATED EGGPLANT & TOFU

1 To prepare the marinade, place all of the ingredients in a small bowl and stir to combine. To prepare the dressing, place all of the ingredients in a separate small bowl and stir to combine. Set the marinade and the dressing aside.

2 To begin preparations for the noodles, trim both ends of the eggplants, slice them in half, and cut them into ½-inch pieces. Place in a mixing bowl, add the marinade, and toss to combine. Let stand for 1 hour at room temperature.

3 Bring a large pot of water to a boil. Add the noodles and stir for the first minute to prevent any sticking. Cook until tender but still chewy, about 3 minutes. Drain, rinse under cold water, drain again, and place in a large bowl. Add the dressing, toss to coat, and set aside.

4 Warm a wok or a large skillet over medium heat for 2 to 3 minutes. Raise heat to medium-high and add 2 tablespoons of the peanut oil. When it begins to shimmer, add the eggplant cubes and a couple pinches of salt and stir-fry until the eggplant softens and starts to brown, 5 to 6 minutes. Using a slotted spoon, transfer the eggplant to a paper towel–lined plate. Add the remaining peanut oil and the tofu cubes to the pan and stir-fry until they turn golden brown all over, 4 to 5 minutes. Using a slotted spoon, transfer the tofu to a separate paper towel–lined plate.

5 Divide the soba noodles between four bowls. Arrange the eggplant and tofu on top and garnish with the scallions.

YIELD: 6 SERVINGS

ACTIVE TIME: 35 MINUTES

TOTAL TIME: 1 HOUR AND 15 MINUTES

CHICKEN WITH 40 CLOVES

8 boneless, skinless chicken thighs

Salt and pepper, to taste

Olive oil, as needed

8 white or baby bella mushrooms, quartered

40 garlic cloves

⅓ cup dry vermouth

¾ cup Chicken Stock (see page 37)

1 tablespoon unsalted butter

1 tablespoon finely chopped fresh tarragon

Buttered egg noodles or white rice, for serving

1 Preheat the oven to 350°F. Generously season the chicken with salt and pepper and put a Dutch oven over high heat. Add the chicken in one layer, cooking in batches if necessary. Although oil is not necessarily needed when cooking chicken thighs, if the pan looks dry add a drizzle of olive oil. When brown on one side, flip to the other side and repeat. Transfer to a plate when fully browned but before they are cooked through.

2 Put the mushrooms in the pot and sauté over medium heat, stirring occasionally, until they are browned all over. Add the garlic and sauté for 1 minute.

3 Add the vermouth and broth to the pot, scrape the browned bits off the bottom of the pot, and then return the chicken to the Dutch oven.

4 Cover the Dutch oven with a lid, place the pot in the oven, and let the chicken braise until the chicken thighs are tender and cooked through, about 25 minutes.

5 Remove from the oven and transfer the chicken and mushrooms to a separate plate. With a fork or large spoon, mash about half of the garlic cloves and stir to incorporate them into the pan sauce. If the sauce is still thin, place the pot over medium-high heat and cook until it has reduced. Return the chicken and mushrooms to the pot, reduce the heat, and cook until warmed through.

6 When ready to serve, add the butter and tarragon to the pot and season to taste. Place one or two thighs and some mushrooms on a plate and spoon the sauce over the top, being sure to include both whole and mashed garlic cloves. Serve with buttered noodles or rice.

FOR THE STEW

8 cups buttermilk

½ cup chickpea flour

1 tablespoon turmeric

1 teaspoon kosher salt

1 tablespoon olive oil

1 teaspoon coriander seeds

1 tablespoon black mustard seeds

2 large yellow onions, halved and sliced thin

6 garlic cloves, minced

2-inch piece of fresh ginger, peeled and minced

1 teaspoon amchoor powder

2 serrano peppers, stemmed, seeds and ribs removed, and minced

FOR THE DUMPLINGS

2 cups spinach, blanched and chopped

2 green serrano peppers, stemmed, seeds and ribs removed, and minced (optional)

2 teaspoons kosher salt

1 teaspoon red pepper flakes

1½ teaspoons chaat masala

1 cup chickpea flour

YIELD: 6 SERVINGS

ACTIVE TIME: 30 MINUTES

TOTAL TIME: 45 MINUTES

SPICED BUTTERMILK STEW WITH SPINACH DUMPLINGS

1   To begin preparations for the stew, place half of the buttermilk, the chickpea flour, turmeric, and salt in a food processor and blitz until smooth. Set the mixture aside.

2   Place the oil in a Dutch oven and warm over high heat. When the oil is shimmering, add the coriander and mustard seeds and cook, while stirring, until they start to pop, about 2 minutes.

3   Reduce the heat to medium and add the onions, garlic, ginger, amchoor powder, and chili peppers. Sauté until the onions start to brown, about 10 minutes, and then pour in the buttermilk mixture. Add the remaining buttermilk, reduce the heat so that the stew gently simmers, and prepare the dumplings.

4   To prepare the dumplings, place the spinach, serrano peppers (if using), salt, red pepper flakes, and chaat masala in a mixing bowl and stir to combine. Add the chickpea flour and stir to incorporate. The dough should be quite stiff.

5   Form tablespoons of the dough into balls and add them to the stew. When all of the dumplings have been added, cover the Dutch oven and simmer over low heat until the dumplings are cooked through, about 10 minutes. Ladle into warmed bowls and serve.

NOTE: Amchoor powder is made from the dried flesh of an unripe mango. Its sour flavor is crucial to North Indian cuisine, and you can find it at better grocery stores or online.

YIELD: 6 SERVINGS

ACTIVE TIME: 45 MINUTES

TOTAL TIME: 5 HOURS

CHICKEN FAJITAS

FOR THE CHICKEN

½ cup orange juice

Juice of 1 lime

4 garlic cloves, minced

1 jalapeño pepper, stemmed, seeds and ribs removed, and diced

2 tablespoons finely chopped fresh cilantro

1 teaspoon cumin

1 teaspoon dried oregano

Salt and pepper, to taste

3 tablespoons olive oil

4 boneless, skinless chicken breasts, sliced into thin strips

FOR THE VEGETABLES

2 tablespoons olive oil

1 red onion, sliced thin

3 bell peppers, stemmed, seeds and ribs removed, and sliced thin

2 jalapeño peppers, stemmed, seeds and ribs removed, and sliced thin

3 garlic cloves, minced

¼ cup fresh lime juice

½ cup fresh cilantro, chopped

Salt and pepper, to taste

Corn Tortillas (see page 77), for serving

Pico de Gallo (see sidebar), for serving

1   To begin preparations for the chicken, place the orange juice, lime juice, garlic, jalapeño, cilantro, cumin, oregano, salt, and pepper in a bowl and stir to combine. Stir in the olive oil, add the chicken, and stir until they are evenly coated. Cover the bowl with plastic wrap and refrigerate for 4 hours.

2   Remove the chicken from the refrigerator and let it come to room temperature.

3   Place a 12-inch cast-iron skillet over medium-high heat. Add the chicken and cook, stirring occasionally, until browned and cooked through, about 8 minutes. Transfer the chicken to a plate and tent with aluminum foil to keep warm.

PICO DE GALLO

Place 4 diced plum tomatoes, 1 diced jalapeño pepper, ½ cup chopped red onion, ¼ cup finely chopped fresh cilantro, and the zest and juice of ½ lime in a mixing bowl and stir to combine. Season with salt to taste and refrigerate for 1 hour before serving.

4   To prepare the vegetables, reduce the heat to medium, add the olive oil to the skillet, and then add the onion, peppers, and garlic. Sauté until the vegetables start to soften, about 5 minutes. Add the lime juice and cilantro, season with salt and pepper, and cook until the vegetables are tender, about 10 minutes.

5   Push the vegetables to one side of the pan and put the chicken on the other side. Serve immediately with the tortillas and Pico de Gallo.

SACHET D'EPICES

Getting familiar with this handy little spice sack will save you a lot of time in a number of preparations. Place 3 sprigs of fresh parsley, 1 sprig of fresh thyme, ½ bay leaf, ¼ teaspoon cracked peppercorns, and ½ garlic clove in a 4-inch square of cheesecloth and fold the corners together to make a purse. Tie it closed with a length of kitchen twine, tie the other end of the twine to the handle of your pan, and drop the sachet into the soup or dish as instructed.

YIELD: 4 SERVINGS

ACTIVE TIME: 30 MINUTES

TOTAL TIME: 1 HOUR AND 35 MINUTES

HAM HOCK & COLLARD GREEN SOUP

16 cups water

1 teaspoon kosher salt

1 lb. collard greens, stemmed and chopped

1 tablespoon olive oil

2 oz. salt pork

½ onion, minced

2 celery stalks, minced

½ cup all-purpose flour

8 cups Chicken Stock (see page 37)

2 smoked ham hocks

Sachet d'Epices (see sidebar)

½ cup heavy cream

1 In a medium saucepan, add the water and salt and bring to a boil. Add the collard greens and cook for 4 minutes, or until they have softened. Remove with a slotted spoon and submerge in ice water. Place on paper towels to dry.

2 In a large saucepan, add the oil and then the salt pork. Cook over medium heat until the salt pork is melted, about 5 minutes. Add the onion and celery and sauté until they have softened, about 5 minutes.

3 Gradually add the flour, stirring constantly, and cook for 4 minutes. Gradually add the stock, stirring constantly to prevent any lumps from forming. Bring to a boil, reduce the heat so that the soup simmers, and add the ham hocks and Sachet d'Epices. Cook for 1 hour.

4 Remove the ham hocks and Sachet d'Epices and add the collard greens to the saucepan. Remove the meat from the ham hocks, mince it, and return it to the soup. Stir in the heavy cream, season to taste, and serve in warm bowls.

YIELD: 4 SERVINGS　　**ACTIVE TIME:** 45 MINUTES　　**TOTAL TIME:** 1 HOUR AND 30 MINUTES

TAGINE WITH PRUNES

3 lbs. bone-in, skin-on chicken thighs

Salt and pepper, to taste

2 tablespoons olive oil, plus more as needed

5 garlic cloves, minced

1¼ teaspoons sweet paprika

½ teaspoon cumin

¼ teaspoon ground ginger

¼ teaspoon coriander

¼ teaspoon cinnamon

¼ teaspoon cayenne pepper

1 tablespoon lemon zest

2 tablespoons honey

1 large onion, sliced

2 carrots, peeled and sliced

2 cups Chicken Stock (see page 37)

2 tablespoons finely chopped fresh parsley, plus more for garnish

1 cup pitted prunes

3 tablespoons fresh lemon juice

1　Pat the chicken dry and season it with salt and pepper. Place the oil in a Dutch oven and warm it over medium-high heat. When the oil starts to shimmer, add the chicken in two batches, cooking until brown on each side, about 8 minutes. Transfer the chicken to a plate and set it aside.

2　Remove all but 1 tablespoon of the rendered fat from the pot. Add all of the remaining ingredients, except for the prunes and lemon juice, and cook until the carrots start to soften, about 8 minutes.

3　Return the chicken to the pot, bring the mixture to a simmer, and then cover the Dutch oven. Reduce the heat to medium-low and simmer the tagine until the chicken is cooked through and tender, about 1 hour.

4　Stir in the prunes and lemon juice, season the tagine with salt and pepper, and serve, garnishing each portion with additional parsley.

FOR THE FILLING

4 cups cold water

¼ cup kosher salt, plus more to taste

1 large eggplant, ends trimmed, cut into cubes

5 tablespoons olive oil

1 lb. ground lamb

1 onion, diced

3 garlic cloves, minced

½ cup dry red wine

1 cup tomato sauce

2 tablespoons finely chopped fresh parsley

1 teaspoon dried oregano

½ teaspoon cinnamon

Black pepper, to taste

FOR THE CRUST

5 eggs

6 tablespoons unsalted butter

⅓ cup all-purpose flour

2½ cups milk

⅔ cup grated Parmesan cheese

⅓ cup chopped fresh dill or parsley, chopped

YIELD: 4 SERVINGS

ACTIVE TIME: 1 HOUR AND 15 MINUTES

TOTAL TIME: 2 HOURS

MOUSSAKA

1   Preheat the oven to 350°F. To begin preparations for the filling, place the cold water in a bowl, add the salt, and stir. When the salt has dissolved, add the eggplant and let it soak for about 20 minutes. Drain the eggplant and rinse with cold water. Squeeze the eggplant to remove as much water as you can, place it on a pile of paper towels, and pat it dry. Set aside.

2   While the eggplant is soaking, place a tablespoon of the olive oil in a large cast-iron skillet and warm it over medium-high heat. When the oil starts to shimmer, add the ground lamb and cook, using a fork to break it up, until it is browned, about 8 minutes. Transfer the cooked lamb to a bowl and set it aside.

3   Add 2 tablespoons of the olive oil and the eggplant to the skillet and cook, stirring frequently until it starts to brown, about 5 minutes. Transfer the cooked eggplant to the bowl containing the lamb and add the rest of the oil, the onion, and the garlic to the skillet. Sauté until the onion is translucent, about 3 minutes, return the lamb and eggplant to the skillet, and stir in the wine, tomato sauce, parsley, oregano,

and cinnamon. Reduce the heat to low and simmer for about 15 minutes, stirring occasionally. Season with salt and pepper and remove the pan from heat.

4   To begin preparations for the crust, place the eggs in a large bowl and beat them lightly. Place a saucepan over medium heat and melt the butter. Reduce the heat to medium-low and add the flour. Stir constantly until the mixture is smooth.

5   While stirring constantly, gradually add the milk and bring the mixture to a boil. When the mixture reaches a boil, remove the pan from heat. Stir approximately half of the mixture in the saucepan into the beaten eggs. Stir the tempered eggs into the saucepan and then add the cheese and dill or parsley. Stir to combine and pour the mixture over the lamb-and-eggplant mixture in the skillet, using a rubber spatula to smooth the top.

6   Place the skillet in the oven and bake until the crust is set and golden brown, about 35 minutes. Remove from the oven and let the moussaka rest for 5 minutes before serving.

THE CENTERPIECES

Dinner is not always a problem that needs to be solved. There are times when it can be used as an expression of passion, a means of marking a moment as something special, a way of celebrating the magic that exists in the homes we've built.

The recipes in this chapter are intended to meet any of those intentions. Some require a bit more time and attention than those occupying the rest of the book, but, of course, there are times when a cold rain has washed away one's grand plans, and a warm kitchen and a day spent preparing something special for those you hold dear are the only acceptable consolations.

Even better: these meals are all substantial enough to provide leftovers for the next night's meal, providing a crucial headstart when the week resumes. And they can all be summoned forth if one needs a dish to dazzle the company that's coming by later on.

CHICKEN BRINE

Place ¾ cup kosher salt, 6 tablespoons sugar, 6 cups room-temperature water, 1½ teaspoons whole black peppercorns, 5 crushed garlic cloves, 3 sprigs of fresh thyme, and 1 bay leaf in a large saucepan and bring the mixture to a boil, stirring to dissolve the sugar and salt. When these are dissolved, remove the pan from heat, transfer the mixture to a stockpot, and add 12 cups ice water and 4 cups ice. Let cool to room temperature before adding the chicken.

YIELD: 4 SERVINGS

ACTIVE TIME: 30 MINUTES

TOTAL TIME: 24 HOURS

ROASTED CHICKEN WITH ROASTED ROOTS & BRASSICAS

1½ gallons Chicken Brine (see sidebar)

5-lb. whole chicken

Salt and pepper, to taste

1 tablespoon finely chopped fresh thyme

1 sweet potato, peeled and chopped

1 cup chopped celery root

2 carrots, peeled and chopped

1 parsnip, trimmed and chopped

2 cups broccoli florets

2 cups cauliflower florets

2 tablespoons olive oil

1   Place the brine in a large stockpot, add the chicken, and place it in the refrigerator overnight. If needed, weigh the chicken down so it is submerged in the brine.

2   Remove the chicken from the brine and discard the brine. Place the chicken on a wire rack resting in a baking sheet and pat as dry as possible. Let sit at room temperature for 1 hour.

3   Preheat the oven to 450°F. Place the chicken in a baking dish, season lightly with salt and pepper, and sprinkle the thyme leaves on top. Place in the oven and roast until the juices run clear and the internal temperature in the thick part of a thigh is 160°F, about 35 minutes. Remove, transfer to a wire rack, and let the chicken rest. Leave the oven on.

4   Place the remaining ingredients in a mixing bowl, season with salt and pepper, and toss to evenly coat. Place on a parchment-lined baking sheet and roast until tender, about 25 minutes. Remove, carve the chicken, and serve alongside the roasted vegetable medley.

YIELD: 6 SERVINGS

ACTIVE TIME: 30 MINUTES

TOTAL TIME: 3 HOURS AND 40 MINUTES

CITRUS & SAGE CHICKEN WITH GOLDEN BEETS

FOR THE MARINADE

3 garlic cloves

⅓ cup fresh sage leaves

Zest and juice of 1 orange

1 tablespoon coriander

½ tablespoon black pepper

½ teaspoon red pepper flakes

¼ cup olive oil

1 tablespoon kosher salt

1 tablespoon minced shallot

FOR THE CHICKEN & BEETS

6 bone-in, skin-on chicken thighs

2 lbs. golden beets, peeled and cut into wedges

2 tablespoons olive oil

Salt and pepper, to taste

1 cup grapefruit juice

4 leeks, white parts only, rinsed well, and sliced thin

1½ shallots, minced

4 tablespoons unsalted butter, cut into 6 pieces

1   To prepare the marinade, place all of the ingredients in a blender and puree until smooth.

2   To begin preparations for the chicken and beets, place the chicken thighs in a resealable plastic bag, pour the marinade over the chicken thighs, and marinate in the refrigerator for 2 hours.

3   Preheat the oven to 375°F. Place the beets in a roasting pan, add the oil, season with salt and pepper, and toss to coat. Add the grapefruit juice, place the pan in the oven, and roast the beets for 50 minutes.

4   Remove the pan from the oven, drain the grapefruit juice, and reserve it. Raise the oven's temperature to 400°F. Add the leeks and shallots to the pan and stir to combine. Push the vegetables to the outside of pan and nestle the chicken thighs, skin side up, in the center. Place in the oven and cook for 40 minutes.

5   Remove the pan from the oven and pour the reserved grapefruit juice over the chicken thighs. Turn the oven to the broiler setting. Place one piece of butter on each piece of chicken, place the pan under the broiler, and broil for 10 minutes, until the chicken is 165°F in the center. The beets should still have a slight snap to them, and the chicken's skin should be crispy.

YIELD: 4 SERVINGS

ACTIVE TIME: 30 MINUTES

TOTAL TIME: 2 HOURS AND 30 MINUTES

CHICKEN VINDALOO

1 tablespoon garam masala

1 teaspoon turmeric

2 teaspoons sweet paprika

1 teaspoon mustard powder

2 tablespoons sugar

1 teaspoon cumin

½ teaspoon cayenne pepper, or to taste

½ cup red wine vinegar

¼ cup tomato paste

5 tablespoons olive oil

3 lbs. chicken pieces

1 large yellow onion, sliced

6 garlic cloves, minced

1-inch piece of fresh ginger, peeled and minced

1 (14 oz.) can of chopped tomatoes, drained

Fresh cilantro, finely chopped, for garnish

1   Place the garam masala, turmeric, paprika, mustard powder, sugar, cumin, cayenne pepper, vinegar, tomato paste, and 2 tablespoons of the olive oil in a mixing bowl and stir to combine. Add the chicken to the mixture, stir until the pieces are evenly coated, cover the bowl, and place it in the refrigerator for 2 hours. If time allows, let the chicken marinate overnight.

2   Place a Dutch oven over medium-high heat and add the remaining oil. When the oil starts to shimmer, add the onion and sauté until it is translucent, about 3 minutes. Reduce the heat to medium, add the garlic and ginger, and sauté for 1 minute.

3   Add the tomatoes, chicken, and marinade to the pot and bring to a boil. Reduce the heat and simmer until the chicken is cooked through, about 18 minutes. Garnish with the cilantro and serve.

YIELD: 4 SERVINGS

ACTIVE TIME: 20 MINUTES

TOTAL TIME: 5 HOURS AND 30 MINUTES

PEPPERED PORK SHOULDER WITH APPLES, CARROTS & ONIONS

1 lb. baby rainbow carrots, halved lengthwise

5 celery stalks, cut into 4-inch-long pieces

2 large yellow onions, quartered

2 Granny Smith apples, cored and cut into wedges

3½-lb. bone-in pork shoulder

1 cinnamon stick

5 garlic cloves, crushed

1 tablespoon kosher salt, plus more to taste

2 tablespoons black pepper

2 tablespoons apple cider vinegar

1½ cups Vegetable or Chicken Stock (see page 22 or 37, respectively)

2 star anise pods

3 bay leaves

1   Place all of the ingredients in a slow cooker, making sure the pork shoulder rests on top of the vegetables. Cover and cook on low until the pork is very tender, about 5 to 6 hours.

2   Remove the cinnamon stick, star anise pods, and bay leaves. Ladle the vegetables and some of the juice into a bowl. Remove the pork shoulder and shred it into large pieces with a fork. To serve, divide the vegetables between the serving plates, place the pork on top, and ladle the juice over each portion.

YIELD: 4 SERVINGS

ACTIVE TIME: 15 MINUTES

TOTAL TIME: 1 HOUR

SPICY LAMB CHOPS WITH RAITA

FOR THE LAMB

3 tablespoons chili powder

3 tablespoons smoked paprika

1 tablespoon dried oregano

2 teaspoons cumin

2 teaspoons black pepper

2 teaspoons kosher salt

1 teaspoon dried thyme

4 lamb chops (each about 1 inch thick)

FOR THE RAITA

1 cup plain yogurt

2 teaspoons minced red onion

½ cup seeded and chopped Persian cucumber

2 tablespoons finely chopped fresh cilantro

1 teaspoon fresh lemon juice

1   To begin preparations for the lamb, place the seasonings in a small bowl and stir to combine. Generously apply the mixture to both sides of the lamb chops, cover the chops with a kitchen towel, and let stand at room temperature for 30 minutes.

2   To prepare the raita, place all of the ingredients in a mixing bowl and stir to combine. Cover the bowl and store in the refrigerator.

3   Preheat your gas or charcoal grill to medium-high heat (450°F). Place the lamb chops on the grill and cook for 3 minutes. Turn the chops over and cook for another 3 minutes for medium-rare, and 4 minutes for medium. The lamb chops should feel slightly firm in the center. Transfer the lamb chops to a cutting board and let them rest for 10 minutes before serving alongside the raita.

YIELD: 4 SERVINGS

ACTIVE TIME: 20 MINUTES

TOTAL TIME: I HOUR

MULLIGATAWNY

4 teaspoons poppy seeds

½ teaspoon cumin seeds

1 teaspoon coriander seeds

¼ teaspoon turmeric

1 yellow onion, chopped

4 garlic cloves, minced

1-inch piece of fresh ginger, peeled and grated

¼ cup olive oil

¾ lb. lamb loin, cut into ½-inch pieces

Pinch of cayenne pepper

4 cups Beef Stock (see page 205) or water

¼ cup long-grain rice

1 tablespoon fresh lemon juice

¼ cup coconut milk

Salt and pepper, to taste

Shredded coconut, for garnish

Fresh cilantro, chopped, for garnish

1 Place the poppy seeds, cumin seeds, and coriander seeds in a dry skillet and toast for 30 seconds over medium heat. Place the toasted seeds, turmeric, onion, garlic, ginger, and 2 tablespoons of the oil in a food processor and blitz until the mixture is a paste. Set the mixture aside.

2 Place the remaining oil in a saucepan and warm it over medium-high heat. When the oil starts to shimmer, add the lamb and sauté until it is browned all over, about 8 minutes. Add the paste and cook for 2 minutes, stirring constantly.

3 Stir in the cayenne pepper and stock or water and bring the soup to a boil. Reduce heat so that the soup simmers, add the rice, and cook until the rice is tender, about 20 minutes.

4 Stir in the lemon juice and coconut milk, season with salt and pepper, and ladle the soup into warmed bowls. Garnish with the coconut and cilantro and serve.

JERK MARINADE

Place ¼ cup maple syrup and brown sugar, 1 tablespoon molasses, fresh lime juice, and finely chopped fresh thyme, ½ teaspoon cayenne pepper, nutmeg, and ground cloves, 1 teaspoon chili powder, paprika, cumin, cinnamon, and black pepper, 2 teaspoons kosher salt and minced fresh ginger, 2 tablespoons sliced scallions and diced shallot, and 2 minced garlic cloves in a food processor and blitz until smooth.

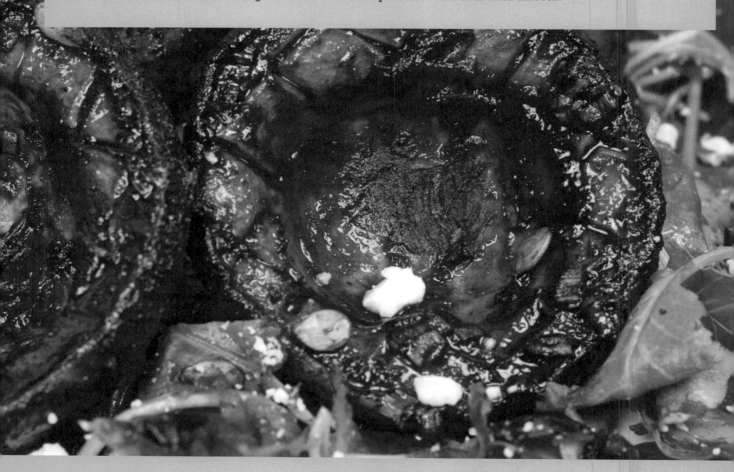

FOR THE SQUASH & SALAD

2 acorn squash

Jerk Marinade (see sidebar)

1 tablespoon olive oil

½ teaspoon kosher salt

¼ teaspoon black pepper

¼ teaspoon paprika

6 cups baby kale

½ cup dried cranberries

4 oz. feta cheese, crumbled

FOR THE MAPLE VINAIGRETTE

½ cup apple cider vinegar

½ cup maple syrup

1 teaspoon orange zest

2 teaspoons Dijon mustard

1 tablespoon kosher salt

1 teaspoon black pepper

2 ice cubes

1½ cups olive oil

YIELD: 4 SERVINGS

ACTIVE TIME: 25 MINUTES

TOTAL TIME: 2 HOURS

JERK ACORN SQUASH WITH BABY KALE SALAD & MAPLE VINAIGRETTE

1   Preheat the oven to 400°F. To begin preparations for the squash and salad, halve the squash lengthwise, remove the seeds, and reserve them. Trim the ends of the squash so that each half can sit evenly, flesh side up, on a baking sheet.

2   Score the squash's flesh in a crosshatch pattern, cutting approximately ⅛ inch into the flesh. Brush some of the marinade on the squash and then fill the cavities with ⅓ cup.

3   Place the baking sheet in the oven and bake until the squash is tender, about 45 minutes to 1 hour. As the squash is cooking, baste the flesh with some of the marinade in the cavity every 15 minutes. Remove from the oven and let cool. Lower the oven's temperature to 350°F.

4   Run the squash seeds under water and remove any pulp. Pat the seeds dry, place them in a mixing bowl, and add the olive oil, salt, pepper, and paprika. Toss to combine and then place the seeds on a baking sheet. Place in the oven and bake until they are light brown and crispy, about 7 minutes.

5   Place the toasted seeds, kale, and cranberries in a salad bowl and toss to combine.

6   To prepare the vinaigrette, place all of the ingredients, except for the olive oil, in a food processor. Turn on high and add the oil in a slow stream. Puree until the mixture has emulsified. Season to taste and add to the salad bowl. Toss to coat and top the salad with the crumbled feta. To serve, place a bed of salad on each plate and place one of the roasted halves of squash on top.

YIELD: 4 SERVINGS

ACTIVE TIME: 15 MINUTES

TOTAL TIME: 5 HOURS

PHO

8 cups Beef Stock (see sidebar)

1 cinnamon stick

4 bay leaves

6 star anise pods

2 teaspoons kosher salt

2 teaspoons peppercorns

2 teaspoons coriander seeds

1 teaspoon allspice berries

1 teaspoon fennel seeds

4-inch piece of fresh ginger, peeled and mashed

6 garlic cloves, smashed

4 lemongrass stalks, bruised

1 white onion, cut into 6 wedges

2 tablespoons dark soy sauce

2 tablespoons rice vinegar

2 tablespoons fish sauce

½ lb. rice noodles

4 baby bok choy, trimmed and quartered

1½ lbs. N.Y. strip steaks

Sriracha, to taste

1½ cups bean sprouts (optional)

2 chili peppers, stemmed, seeds and ribs removed, and sliced (optional)

Fresh cilantro, torn (optional)

Fresh Thai basil leaves (optional)

Scallions, trimmed and chopped (optional)

Lime wedges (optional)

1   Place all of the ingredients preceding the rice noodles in a slow cooker, cover, and cook on low for at least 4 hours. If time allows, cook for 8 hours, which will produce and extremely flavorful broth.

2   Strain the broth through a fine sieve. Discard the solids and return the broth to the slow cooker. Add the noodles and bok choy to the broth, cover, and cook on low for approximately 30 minutes, until the noodles are tender and the bok choy is al dente.

3   Slice the steak into ⅛-inch-thick pieces. Ladle the broth, noodles, and bok choy into bowls and top with the steak. The broth will cook the steak to rare. If you prefer the steak to be cooked more, add the slices to the slow cooker and cook in the broth for 2 to 3 minutes for medium-rare, and 3 to 5 minutes for medium. Season with sriracha and tailor your bowl to taste with bean sprouts, chili peppers, cilantro, Thai basil, scallions, and lime wedges.

BEEF STOCK

Place 7 lbs. beef bones in a stockpot and cover with cold water. Bring to a simmer over medium-high heat, skimming to remove any impurities that float to the surface. Reduce the heat to low, add 2 chopped yellow onions, 3 chopped carrots, 4 chopped celery stalks, 3 crushed garlic cloves, 3 sprigs of fresh thyme, 1 teaspoon whole black peppercorns, and 1 bay leaf, and simmer for 5 hours, skimming to remove any impurities that float to the surface. Strain, let cool slightly, and transfer to the refrigerator. Leave uncovered and let cool completely. Remove the layer of fat and cover. The stock will keep in the refrigerator for 3 to 5 days, and in the freezer for up to 3 months.

FOR THE BBQ SAUCE

½ cup ketchup

¼ cup dark brown sugar

2 tablespoons granulated sugar

2 tablespoons Dijon mustard

3 tablespoons apple cider vinegar

2 garlic cloves, minced

¼ cup blackstrap molasses

¼ teaspoon ground cloves

½ teaspoon hot sauce

¼ cup honey

FOR THE RIBS

10 lbs. St. Louis-cut pork ribs

½ cup kosher salt

2 tablespoons light brown sugar

2 tablespoons garlic powder

1 tablespoon onion powder

1 tablespoon chili powder

1 tablespoon paprika

1 tablespoon cumin

2 cups applewood chips

8 cups apple juice or apple cider

YIELD: 10 SERVINGS

ACTIVE TIME: 45 MINUTES

TOTAL TIME: 5 HOURS AND 30 MINUTES

APPLEWOOD-SMOKED RIBS WITH MOLASSES BBQ SAUCE

1   To prepare the BBQ sauce, place all of the ingredients in a medium saucepan and bring to a boil over medium-high heat. Reduce heat so that the sauce simmers and cook, stirring occasionally, until the sauce has reduced by one-third, about 20 minutes. Remove the pan from heat and set the sauce aside.

2   To begin preparations for the ribs, place the ribs in a roasting pan. Place all of the remaining ingredients, except for the wood chips and the apple juice or apple cider, in a bowl and stir until combined.

3   Rub the mixture in the bowl all over the ribs, making sure every inch is covered. Place the ribs in the refrigerator for 1 hour.

4   Heat your smoker to 250°F and place the BBQ sauce beside it. Once it reaches the desired temperature, add the applewood chips and 1 cup of apple juice or cider to the steam tray. Place the ribs in the smoker and cook, while brushing the ribs with the sauce every 30

minutes, for about 4 hours, until the meat begins to pull away from the bones. While the ribs are cooking, make sure you keep an eye on the steam tray and continue refilling it with apple juice or cider. You do not want the steam tray to be dry for any length of time.

5   When the ribs have finished cooking, remove them from the smoker, wrap them in aluminum foil, and let them rest for 20 minutes before serving.

NOTE: If you do not have a smoker, you can still prepare this dish on your grill. Soak the applewood chips in apple juice or apple cider for 1 hour before grilling and either place them on the coals or, if using a gas grill, into a smoker box before placing the ribs on the grill.

YIELD: 6 SERVINGS

ACTIVE TIME: 1 HOUR

TOTAL TIME: 2 HOURS AND 30 MINUTES

SWEET POTATO GNOCCHI WITH SAGE BROWN BUTTER

2½ lbs. sweet potatoes

½ cup ricotta cheese

1 egg

2 egg yolks

1 tablespoon kosher salt, plus more to taste

1 teaspoon black pepper

3 tablespoons light brown sugar

2 tablespoons real maple syrup

2 cups all-purpose flour, plus more as needed

1 cup semolina flour

2 tablespoons olive oil

1 stick of unsalted butter

1 tablespoon finely chopped fresh sage

2 cups arugula

½ cup walnuts, toasted and chopped

1 Preheat the oven to 350°F. Wash the sweet potatoes, place them on a parchment-lined baking sheet, and use a knife to pierce several holes in the tops of the potatoes. Place in the oven and cook until they are fork-tender all the way through, 45 minutes to 1 hour. Remove from the oven, slice them open, and let them cool completely.

2 Scrape the cooled sweet potato flesh into a mixing bowl and mash until smooth. Add the ricotta, egg, egg yolks, salt, pepper, brown sugar, and maple syrup and stir until thoroughly combined. Add the flours 1 cup at a time and work the mixture with your hands until incorporated. The dough should not feel sticky when touched. If it is too sticky, add more all-purpose flour 1 teaspoon at a time until it has the right texture. Place the olive oil in a mixing bowl and set aside.

3 Transfer the dough to a lightly floured work surface and cut it into 10 even pieces. Roll each piece into a long rope and cut the ropes into ¾-inch-long pieces. Use a fork to roll the gnocchi into the desired shapes and place the shaped dumplings on a lightly floured baking sheet.

4   Bring a large pot of salted water to boil. Working in small batches, add the gnocchi to the boiling water and stir to keep them from sticking to the bottom. The gnocchi will eventually float to the surface. Cook for 1 more minute, remove, and transfer to the bowl containing the olive oil. Toss to coat and transfer on a parchment-lined baking sheet to cool.

5   Place the butter in a skillet and cook over medium heat until it begins to brown. Add the sage and cook until the bubbles start to dissipate. Place the arugula in a bowl and set aside.

6   Working in batches, add the gnocchi to the skillet, stir to coat, and cook until they have a nice sear on one side. Transfer to the bowl of arugula and toss to combine. Serve and top each portion with the toasted walnuts.

YIELD: 4 SERVINGS

ACTIVE TIME: 30 MINUTES

TOTAL TIME: 8 HOURS AND 30 MINUTES

BEEF STEW

1½ lbs. beef chuck, cut into 1-inch pieces

2 tablespoons kosher salt

1 tablespoon black pepper

1 tablespoon onion powder

1 tablespoon garlic powder

½ tablespoon dried oregano

1 teaspoon celery seeds

Pinch of red pepper flakes

2 tablespoons finely chopped fresh thyme

2 bay leaves

4 cups Beef Stock (see page 205)

3 garlic cloves, minced

3 carrots, peeled and chopped

2 leeks, trimmed, rinsed well, and chopped

1 yellow onion, chopped

2 Yukon Gold potatoes, peeled and chopped

2 celery stalks, chopped

3 tablespoons tomato paste

2 tablespoons Worcestershire sauce

1 tablespoon soy sauce

¼ cup all-purpose flour

Fresh parsley, finely chopped, for garnish

1 Place all of the ingredients, except for 1 cup of the stock, the flour, and the parsley, in a slow cooker and stir to combine.

2 Place the flour and remaining stock in a bowl and stir until the mixture is smooth. Add this mixture to the slow cooker and cover. Cook on low until the beef and potatoes are extremely tender, about 8 hours. Ladle into warmed bowls and garnish each portion with parsley.

YIELD: 6 SERVINGS

ACTIVE TIME: 15 MINUTES

TOTAL TIME: 8 HOURS AND 15 MINUTES

MOROCCAN LENTIL STEW

1 cup brown lentils

½ cup green lentils

4 cups Vegetable Stock (see page 22)

3 carrots, peeled and chopped

1 large yellow onion, peeled and chopped

3 garlic cloves, minced

3-inch piece of fresh ginger, peeled and minced

Zest and juice of 1 lemon

3 tablespoons smoked paprika

2 tablespoons cinnamon

1 tablespoon coriander

1 tablespoon turmeric

1 tablespoon cumin

1½ teaspoons allspice

2 bay leaves

Salt and pepper, to taste

1 (14 oz.) can of cannellini beans, drained and rinsed

Fresh mint, finely chopped, for garnish

Goat cheese, crumbled, for garnish

1 Place the lentils in a fine sieve and rinse them to remove any impurities. Place all of the ingredients, save the cannellini beans and the garnishes, in a slow cooker. Cover and cook on low for 7½ hours.

2 After 7½ hours, stir in the cannellini beans. Cover and cook on low for 30 another minutes. Ladle into warmed bowls and garnish with fresh mint and goat cheese.

YIELD: 4 SERVINGS

ACTIVE TIME: 40 MINUTES

TOTAL TIME: 2 HOURS

RATATOUILLE

⅓ cup olive oil

6 garlic cloves, minced

1 eggplant, chopped

2 zucchini, sliced into half-moons

2 bell peppers, stemmed, seeds and ribs removed, and chopped

4 tomatoes, seeded and chopped

Salt and pepper, to taste

1 Place a large cast-iron skillet over medium-high heat and add half of the olive oil. When the oil starts to shimmer, add the garlic and eggplant and sauté until pieces are coated with oil and just starting to sizzle, about 2 minutes.

2 Reduce the heat to medium and stir in the zucchini, peppers, and remaining oil. Cover the skillet and cook, stirring occasionally, until the eggplant, zucchini, and peppers are almost tender, about 15 minutes.

3 Add the tomatoes, stir to combine, and cook until the eggplant, zucchini, and peppers are tender and the tomatoes have collapsed, about 25 minutes. Remove the skillet from heat, season with salt and pepper, and allow to sit for at least 1 hour. Reheat before serving.

YIELD: 4 SERVINGS

ACTIVE TIME: 30 MINUTES

TOTAL TIME: 1 HOUR

HALIBUT WITH BRAISED VEGETABLES

¼ cup olive oil

1 yellow bell pepper, stemmed, seeds and ribs removed, and chopped

1 red bell pepper, stemmed, seeds and ribs removed, and chopped

1 habanero pepper, pierced

2 small white sweet potatoes, peeled and chopped

1 cup diced red cabbage

Salt and pepper, to taste

3 graffiti eggplants, chopped

2-inch piece of fresh ginger, peeled and mashed

4 garlic cloves, minced

2 tablespoons green curry paste

3 baby bok choy, chopped

4 cups Fish Stock (see sidebar)

2 tablespoons sweet paprika

2 tablespoons finely chopped fresh cilantro

3 (14 oz.) cans of coconut milk

2 bunches of Tuscan kale, stemmed and torn

1½ lbs. halibut fillets

Scallions, trimmed and chopped, for garnish

1   Place the olive oil in a Dutch oven and warm it over medium-high heat. When the oil starts to shimmer, add the bell peppers, habanero pepper, sweet potatoes, and cabbage. Season with salt and pepper and sauté until the sweet potatoes begin to caramelize, about 6 minutes.

2   Add the eggplants, ginger, and garlic and sauté until the eggplants begin to collapse, about 10 minutes. Stir in the curry paste and cook until the mixture is fragrant, about 2 minutes.

3   Add the bok choy, stock, paprika, cilantro, and coconut milk and cook until the liquid has reduced by one-quarter, about 20 minutes.

4   Add the kale to the Dutch oven. Place the halibut fillets on top of the kale, reduce the heat to medium, cover, and cook until the fish is cooked through, about 10 minutes.

5   Remove the Dutch oven's cover, remove the habanero, and discard it. Ladle the vegetables and the sauce into the bowls and top each one with a halibut fillet. Garnish with the scallions and serve.

FISH STOCK

Place ¼ cup olive oil in a stockpot and warm over low heat. Add 1 trimmed, rinsed, and chopped leek, 1 unpeeled, chopped onion, 2 chopped carrots, and 1 chopped celery stalk and cook until the liquid they release has evaporated. Add ¾ lb. of whitefish bodies, 4 sprigs of fresh parsley, 3 sprigs of fresh thyme, 2 bay leaves, 1 teaspoon of black peppercorns and salt, and 8 cups water, raise the heat to high, and bring to a boil. Reduce heat so that the stock simmers and cook for 3 hours, while skimming to remove any impurities that float to the surface. Strain the stock through a fine sieve, let it cool slightly, and place in the refrigerator, uncovered, to chill. When the stock is completely cool, remove the fat layer from the top and cover. The stock will keep in the refrigerator for 3 to 5 days, and in the freezer for up to 3 months.

YIELD: 6 SERVINGS

ACTIVE TIME: 25 MINUTES

TOTAL TIME: 7 HOURS

CHICKEN & SAUSAGE CACCIATORE

1 lb. sweet Italian sausage

2 lbs. boneless, skinless chicken thighs

1 (28 oz.) can of whole San Marzano tomatoes, drained

1 (28 oz.) can of diced tomatoes, drained

⅔ cup dry red wine

4 shallots, chopped

3 garlic cloves, minced

1 green bell pepper, stemmed, seeds and ribs removed, and chopped

1 orange bell pepper, stemmed, seeds and ribs removed, and chopped

1 tablespoon garlic powder

1 tablespoon sugar

2 tablespoons kosher salt, plus more to taste

½ teaspoon red pepper flakes

1 cup white rice

Black pepper, to taste

1 tablespoon finely chopped fresh oregano, for garnish

Parmesan cheese, grated, for garnish

1   Place all of the ingredients, except for the white rice, black pepper, and the garnishes, in a slow cooker. Cook on low for 5½ hours.

2   Add the rice to the slow cooker, raise the heat to high, and cook until the rice is tender, 40 to 50 minutes. The cooking time may vary depending on your slow cooker, so be sure to check on the rice after about 30 minutes to avoid overcooking.

3   Season with salt and pepper, garnish with the oregano and a generous amount of Parmesan, and serve.

YIELD: 6 SERVINGS

ACTIVE TIME: 15 MINUTES

TOTAL TIME: 9 HOURS

COFFEE & BOURBON BRISKET

FOR THE BRISKET

1 yellow onion, chopped

1 peach, peeled, pitted, and chopped

1 nectarine, peeled, pitted, and chopped

2-inch piece of fresh ginger, peeled and minced

½ cup Dry Rub (see sidebar)

3½ lbs. flat-cut brisket

1 cup water

FOR THE BBQ SAUCE

2 cups brewed coffee

¼ cup dark brown sugar

¾ cup bourbon

3 tablespoons molasses

¼ cup apple cider vinegar

2 tablespoons Worcestershire sauce

¼ cup ketchup

1 tablespoon garlic powder

½ tablespoon black pepper

1 tablespoon cornstarch

1 To prepare the brisket, place the onion, peach, nectarine, and ginger in a slow cooker. Apply the Dry Rub to the brisket and place the brisket on top of the mixture in the slow cooker. Add the water, cover, and cook on low for 6 hours.

2 Remove the contents of the slow cooker, transfer the brisket to a cutting board, and discard everything else. Place all of the ingredients for the BBQ sauce in the slow cooker and cook on high for 1 hour.

3 Return the brisket to the slow cooker, reduce the heat to low, and cook for another hour. Remove the brisket from the slow cooker, let it rest for 30 minutes, and then use a sharp knife to cut it into ½-inch-thick slices, making sure to cut against the grain.

DRY RUB

Place ¼ cup ground coffee, 1 teaspoon coriander, 2 teaspoons black pepper, a pinch of red pepper flakes, 1 teaspoon cumin, 2 teaspoons mustard powder, 2 teaspoons dark chili powder, 1 teaspoon paprika, 6 tablespoons kosher salt, and 6 tablespoons light brown sugar in a mixing bowl and stir to combine. Store in an airtight container for up to 6 months.

YIELD: 4 SERVINGS

ACTIVE TIME: 30 MINUTES

TOTAL TIME: 4 HOURS AND 30 MINUTES

YANKEE SHORT RIBS

2 tablespoons olive oil

4 lbs. short ribs

Salt and pepper, to taste

2 large onions, sliced

4 carrots, peeled and diced

4 large potatoes, peeled and diced

8 cups Beef Stock (see page 205)

4 bay leaves

2 sprigs of fresh rosemary

2 sprigs of fresh thyme

½ cup red wine

1 Preheat the oven to 300°F. Place the oil in a large skillet and warm it over medium-high heat. Pat the short ribs dry and season them generously with salt. Working in batches, place the short ribs in the skillet and cook, while turning, until they are browned all over.

2 Place the browned short ribs in a Dutch oven along with the onions, carrots, potatoes, stock, and bay leaves. Cover, place in the oven, and cook until the short ribs are fork-tender and the meat easily comes away from the bone, about 4 hours. Remove from the oven, strain through a fine sieve, and reserve the cooking liquid.

3 Place the reserved liquid in a pan with the rosemary, thyme, and red wine. Cook over high heat until the mixture has reduced and started to thicken. Season with salt and pepper. Divide the short ribs and vegetables between the serving plates and spoon 2 to 3 tablespoons of the sauce over each portion.

YIELD: 6 SERVINGS

ACTIVE TIME: 15 MINUTES

TOTAL TIME: 45 MINUTES

CAPRESE CHICKEN

1 garlic clove, minced

1 teaspoon dried oregano

1 teaspoon garlic powder

Salt and pepper, to taste

2 tablespoons olive oil

2 lbs. boneless, skinless chicken breasts, halved along their equators

1 lb. tomatoes, sliced

1 lb. fresh mozzarella cheese, drained and sliced

Leaves from 1 bunch of fresh basil

Balsamic glaze, for garnish

1 Preheat the oven to 375°F. Place the minced garlic, oregano, garlic powder, salt, and pepper in a bowl and stir to combine. Place 1 tablespoon of the olive oil and the sliced chicken breasts in a bowl and toss to coat. Dredge the chicken breasts in the garlic-and-spice mixture and set aside.

2 Coat the bottom of a large cast-iron skillet with the remaining oil and warm over medium-high heat. Working in batches, sear the chicken breasts for 1 minute on each side.

3 When all of the chicken has been seared, place half of the breasts in an even layer on the bottom of the skillet. Top with two-thirds of the tomatoes and mozzarella and half of the basil leaves. Place the remaining chicken breasts on top in an even layer and cover it with the remaining tomatoes, mozzarella, and basil.

4 Place the skillet in the oven and cook until the interior temperature of the chicken breasts is 165°F, about 10 minutes. Remove the skillet from the oven and let rest for 10 minutes. Drizzle the balsamic glaze over the top and serve.

FOR THE MARINADE

2 tablespoons finely chopped fresh thyme

2 habanero peppers, stemmed, seeds and ribs removed, and chopped

½ yellow onion

½ cup brown sugar

½ tablespoon cinnamon

½ teaspoon grated fresh nutmeg

1 tablespoon allspice

2-inch piece of fresh ginger, peeled and minced

1 cup olive oil

2 tablespoons soy sauce

1 scallion, trimmed and chopped

1 tablespoon kosher salt

1 tablespoon black pepper

1 tablespoon rice vinegar

FOR THE CHICKEN & VEGETABLES

5 lbs. bone-in, skin-on chicken pieces

3 red beets, peeled and chopped

3 carrots, peeled and chopped

1 large sweet potato, peeled and chopped

3 turnips, peeled and chopped

¼ cup olive oil

Salt and pepper, to taste

2 tablespoons finely chopped fresh thyme

YIELD: 6 SERVINGS

ACTIVE TIME: 15 MINUTES

TOTAL TIME: 24 HOURS

JERK CHICKEN WITH VEGETABLES

1   To prepare the marinade, place all of the ingredients in a blender and blend until smooth.

2   To begin preparations for the chicken and vegetables, place the chicken in a large baking pan, pour the marinade over the chicken, and refrigerate overnight.

3   Preheat the oven to 375°F. Place the vegetables, oil, salt, and pepper in an 9 x 13–inch baking pan and roast for 30 minutes. Remove, add the thyme, return the pan to the oven, and roast for an additional 25 minutes. While the vegetables are roasting, remove the chicken from the refrigerator and let it come to room temperature.

4   Remove the pan from the oven. Shake the chicken to remove any excess marinade and then place the chicken on top of the vegetables. Return the pan to the oven and roast for 45 to 50 minutes, until the interiors of thickest parts of the chicken reach 165°F. Remove the pan from the oven and serve immediately.

YIELD: 4 SERVINGS

ACTIVE TIME: 30 MINUTES

TOTAL TIME: I HOUR

PORK & APPLE CASSEROLE

8 apples, cored and sliced

2 teaspoons cinnamon

1 teaspoon grated fresh nutmeg

¼ cup sugar

¼ cup all-purpose flour

Salt and pepper, to taste

¼ cup apple cider

1½-lb. pork tenderloin

2 tablespoons ground fresh rosemary

2 tablespoons ground fresh thyme

1   Preheat the oven to 325°F. Place the apples, cinnamon, nutmeg, sugar, flour, and a pinch of salt in a mixing bowl and stir to combine. Transfer the mixture to a baking dish or Dutch oven and then add the apple cider.

2   Rub the pork tenderloin with the ground herbs and a pinch of salt. Place the pork on top of the apple mixture, cover, and place in the oven. Cook until a meat thermometer inserted into the center of the tenderloin registers 145°F, about 40 minutes.

3   Remove the pork tenderloin from the oven and let it rest for 10 minutes. Slice it thin and serve on beds of the apple mixture.

YIELD: 4 SERVINGS

ACTIVE TIME: 30 MINUTES

TOTAL TIME: 4 HOURS

BRAISED LAMB WITH MINTY PEAS

2 tablespoons olive oil

5-lb. bone-in lamb shoulder

Salt, to taste

1 small onion, diced

2 carrots, peeled and diced

3 bay leaves

2 tablespoons black peppercorns

2 cups water

2 sprigs of fresh rosemary

3 sprigs of fresh mint

3 cups peas

1   Preheat the oven to 300°F. Place the oil in a Dutch oven and warm it over medium-high heat. Season all sides of the lamb shoulder generously with salt. When the oil starts to shimmer, place the lamb in the pan and cook, turning occasionally, until it is browned on all sides.

2   Place the onion, carrots, bay leaves, peppercorns, water, and rosemary in the Dutch oven. Cover, place in the oven, and braise until the lamb is extremely tender, about 3½ hours.

3   When the lamb shoulder is close to ready, place the mint and peas in a saucepan and cover with water. Cook over medium heat until the peas are tender, approximately 4 minutes for fresh peas and 7 minutes if using frozen. Drain, discard the mint, and serve the peas alongside the lamb shoulder.

YIELD: 6 SERVINGS

ACTIVE TIME: 45 MINUTES

TOTAL TIME: 3 HOURS AND 30 MINUTES

GRILLED LAMB LOIN WITH QUINOA & RADISH LEAF CHIMICHURRI

FOR THE LAMB & QUINOA

2½-lb. lamb loin

Lamb Marinade (see sidebar)

2 cups quinoa, rinsed

4½ cups water

1 small shallot, trimmed and halved

2 teaspoons kosher salt, plus more to taste

6 baby bok choy, trimmed

10 radishes, trimmed and quartered, tops reserved

Black pepper, to taste

2 tablespoons fresh lemon juice

FOR THE CHIMICHURRI

1 small shallot, minced

2 garlic cloves, minced

¼ teaspoon red pepper flakes

¼ cup red wine vinegar

⅔ cup finely chopped radish leaves

1 tablespoon finely chopped fresh oregano

½ cup olive oil

2 teaspoons kosher salt, plus more to taste

1 To begin preparations for the lamb and quinoa, trim the fat from the lamb loin. Place it in a bowl, rub it with the marinade, and let it marinate in the refrigerator for at least 2 hours. Remove approximately 45 minutes prior to grilling.

2 Place the quinoa in a medium saucepan and cover with the water. Add the shallot and salt and bring to a boil. Cover the pan and lower the temperature so that the quinoa simmers. Cook until the quinoa has absorbed all of the liquid, about 20 minutes. Remove the shallot, spread the quinoa in an even layer on a parchment-lined baking sheet, and let it cool.

3 Bring a pot of water to a boil and prepare an ice water bath. Add salt to the water, rinse the bok choy under cold water, and place it in the boiling water. Cook for 1 minute, remove with a strainer, and transfer to the ice water bath.

4 Let the water come back to a boil and then add the radish tops. Cook for 1 minute, remove with a strainer, and transfer to the ice water bath. When the vegetables have cooled completely, drain, pat dry, and place them in a mixing bowl. Season with salt and pepper, add the quartered radishes and lemon juice, and toss to evenly coat. Set aside.

5 Preheat your gas or charcoal grill to medium-high heat (about 450°F). Place the lamb loin on the grill and cook, while turning, until seared on all sides and the internal temperature is 140°F. Remove from the grill and let the lamb rest for 10 minutes before slicing.

6 To prepare the chimichurri, place all of the ingredients in a mixing bowl and whisk until combined. Season to taste and set aside.

7 To serve, place the quinoa and vegetables on a plate and top with slices of the lamb. Drizzle the chimichurri over each portion or serve it on the side.

NOTE: This chimichurri sauce can be prepared with fresh parsley standing in for the radish leaves, and is wonderful over grilled steak.

LAMB MARINADE

Place 8 minced garlic cloves, 1 tablespoon cumin, 2 tablespoons black pepper, 1 tablespoon ground fennel, 1 tablespoon paprika, 2 tablespoons kosher salt, 2 teaspoons Dijon mustard, and 1 cup olive oil in a mixing bowl and stir until combined.

1½ cups all-purpose flour, plus
more as needed

1½ teaspoons kosher salt, plus
more to taste

¾ cup egg yolks

1 tablespoon olive oil

1 bunch of asparagus, trimmed
and chopped

½ lb. snap peas, trimmed and
chopped

4 tablespoons unsalted butter

¼ cup grated Parmesan cheese

½ teaspoon red pepper flakes

YIELD: 4 SERVINGS

ACTIVE TIME: 50 MINUTES

TOTAL TIME: I HOUR AND 30 MINUTES

TAGLIATELLE WITH ASPARAGUS & PEAS

1   Place the flour and salt in a mixing bowl, stir to combine, and make a well in the center. Add the egg yolks and olive oil to the well and, starting in the center and gradually working to the outside, incorporate the flour into the well. When all the flour has been incorporated, place the dough on a lightly floured work surface and knead it until it is a smooth ball. Cover the dough with plastic wrap and let it rest for 30 minutes.

2   Divide the dough into quarters. Use a rolling pin to flatten each quarter to a thickness that can go through the widest setting on a pasta maker.

3   Run the rolled pieces of dough through the pasta maker, adjusting the setting to reduce the thickness with each pass. Roll until you can see your hand through the dough. Cut the sheets into 10-inch-long pieces, dust each one with flour, stack them on top of each other, and gently roll them up. Cut the roll into ¼-inch-wide strips, unroll, and place the strips on baking sheets lightly dusted with flour.

4   Bring water to a boil in a medium saucepan and also in a large saucepan. Add salt to each of the saucepans once the water is boiling. Place the asparagus and peas in the medium saucepan and cook for 1 minute. Drain and set aside.

5   Place the pasta in the large saucepan and cook for 3 to 4 minutes, stirring constantly. Reserve ¼ cup of the pasta water and then drain the pasta.

6   Place the butter in a large skillet and melt over medium heat. Add the pasta and vegetables and toss to combine. Add the reserved pasta water, Parmesan, and red pepper flakes and toss to evenly coat. Season to taste and serve.

NOTE: If you don't have a pasta maker, roll out the dough as thin as it can get on a flour-dusted work surface and then cut it into 10-inch-long and ¼-inch-wide strips.

YIELD: 6 SERVINGS

ACTIVE TIME: I HOUR AND 30 MINUTES

TOTAL TIME: 24 HOURS

BRAISED PORK BELLY WITH TOASTED FARRO

2 cups farro

3 ears of corn, husked and rinsed

4-lb. skin-on pork belly

1 tablespoon kosher salt, plus more to taste

Black pepper, to taste

2 tablespoons olive oil

2 large yellow onions, chopped

2 large carrots, peeled and chopped

4 celery stalks, chopped

6 garlic cloves, crushed

6 sprigs of fresh thyme

3 tablespoons tomato paste

2 cups white wine

8 cups Chicken Stock (see page 37)

6 cups water

1 shallot, halved

1 bay leaf

4 oz. snap peas, trimmed and chopped

4 tablespoons unsalted butter

¼ cup finely chopped fresh chives

1   The night before you are going to serve this preparation, preheat the oven to 350°F and place the farro on a rimmed baking sheet in an even layer. Place it in the oven and bake until the farro is a deep brown color. Remove from the oven, place it in a bowl, factoring in that the grains will double in size, and cover with the water. Soak overnight.

2   Preheat the oven to 350°F. Place the ears of corn in the oven and cook until the kernels give slightly when squeezed. Remove from the oven and let cool. Lower the oven temperature to 250°F.

3   Place the pork belly skin side down on a work surface and use a knife to score the flesh, slicing ¼ inch deep in a crosshatch pattern. Season with salt and pepper and set aside.

4 Place the olive oil in a large Dutch oven and warm over high heat. When the oil starts to shimmer, carefully place the pork belly, skin side down, in the pot to begin rendering the fat. Sear until the skin is brown, turn over, and sear until brown on this side. Remove the pork belly from the pot and set it aside.

5 Add the onions, carrots, celery, and garlic to the Dutch oven and sauté until the onion starts to brown, about 8 minutes. Add 4 sprigs of the thyme and the tomato paste, stir to coat the vegetables, and then add the wine. Scrape up any browned bits from the bottom of the Dutch oven and cook until the liquid starts to thicken. Add the stock, bring to a boil, and return the pork belly to the pot. Cover the Dutch oven and transfer it to the oven. Cook until the pork belly is very tender, 2 to 2½ hours.

6 When the pork belly is tender, strain and reserve the liquid, discard the vegetables, set the pork belly aside, and place the liquid in a saucepan. Cook over high heat until it is thick and syrupy. Set aside.

7 Drain the farro and place it in a large pot with the water, shallot, 1 tablespoon salt, remaining sprigs of thyme, and the bay leaf. Bring to a boil over medium-high heat and then reduce the heat so that the mixture simmers. Cook until the farro is al dente, about 20 minutes. Remove the shallot, thyme, and bay leaf, drain, and transfer the farro to a bowl.

8 Remove the kernels from the roasted ears of corn. Bring a small pot of water to a boil, add salt and the snap peas, and cook for 1 minute. Drain and add to the farro along with the corn, butter, and chives. Stir to combine, season with salt and pepper, and transfer to a serving dish.

9 Slice the pork belly and place the slices on top of the farro-and-corn mixture. Spoon the reduced cooking liquid over the top and serve.

6- to 8-lb., bone-in pork shoulder

Salt and pepper, to taste

1 large yellow onion, chopped

3 bay leaves

2 teaspoons paprika

¼ cup brown sugar

2 tablespoons black peppercorns

7 cups Chicken Stock (see page 37)

1 tablespoon Dijon mustard

2 cups medium-grain cornmeal

2 cups water

1 stick of unsalted butter

1 cup crumbled blue cheese

8 overly ripe peaches, pitted and quartered

2 cups apple cider vinegar

¾ cup sugar

3 garlic cloves, chopped

6 jalapeño peppers, stemmed, seeds and ribs removed, and diced

4 cayenne peppers, stemmed, seeds and ribs removed, and diced

¼ cup fresh lemon juice

YIELD: 6 SERVINGS

ACTIVE TIME: 1 HOUR

TOTAL TIME: 5 HOURS

PORK WITH BLUE CHEESE POLENTA & ROASTED PEACH HOT SAUCE

1 Preheat the oven to 300°F. Season the pork generously with salt, place it in a large skillet, and cook, turning as it browns, over medium-high heat until browned all over.

2 Transfer the pork shoulder to a Dutch oven and add the onion, bay leaves, paprika, brown sugar, peppercorns, 4 cups of the stock, and the mustard.

3 Cover the Dutch oven, place it in the oven, and cook until the pork is extremely tender, about 4 hours. Remove from the oven, let cool slightly, and then shred the pork shoulder with a fork.

4 Approximately 1 hour before the pulled pork will be finished cooking, place the cornmeal, the remaining stock, and the water in a large pot. Bring to a boil over medium-high heat, reduce the heat so that the mixture simmers, and cook, stirring frequently, until the mixture is thick and creamy, about 40 minutes to 1 hour.

5 Stir half of the butter and half of the blue cheese into the polenta. Season it with salt and pepper, remove the pan from heat, and set it aside.

6 Once you have removed the pork shoulder from the oven, raise the oven temperature to 400°F. Place the peaches flesh side up on a baking sheet and place them in the oven. Cook until they began to darken, about 10 minutes. You can also grill the peaches if you're after a slightly smokier sauce.

7 Remove the peaches from the oven and place them in a medium saucepan. Add the vinegar, sugar, garlic, and peppers and bring to a simmer over medium-low heat. Simmer for 10 minutes, transfer the mixture to a blender, and puree until smooth. Set the hot sauce aside.

8 Stir the remaining butter into the polenta and then spoon the polenta into warmed bowls. Top each portion with some of the pulled pork, hot sauce, and remaining blue cheese.

YIELD: 4 SERVINGS

ACTIVE TIME: 25 MINUTES

TOTAL TIME: I HOUR

CHICKEN THIGHS WITH TABBOULEH

FOR THE TABBOULEH

1 cup bulgur wheat

2 cups water

1 shallot, halved

2 sprigs of fresh thyme

1 tablespoon kosher salt, plus more to taste

1 tablespoon finely chopped fresh cilantro

1 tablespoon finely chopped fresh parsley

1 scallion, trimmed and minced

1½ tablespoons fresh lime juice

½ cup minced tomato

½ cup minced cucumber

1 garlic clove, minced

3 tablespoons olive oil

Black pepper, to taste

FOR THE CHICKEN THIGHS

2 tablespoons olive oil

Salt and pepper, to taste

2 teaspoons paprika

2 teaspoons cumin

2 teaspoons ground fennel

4 bone-in, skin-on chicken thighs

1 cup cherry tomatoes

2 garlic cloves, crushed

1 shallot, sliced

½ cup white wine

1   To prepare the tabbouleh, place the bulgur, water, shallot, thyme, and salt in a saucepan and bring to a boil. Remove from heat, cover the pan with foil, and let sit until the bulgur has absorbed all the liquid. Fluff with a fork, remove the shallot and thyme, and add the remaining ingredients. Season with salt and pepper and stir to combine. Set the tabbouleh aside.

2   To begin preparations for the chicken thighs, preheat the oven to 450°F. Place the olive oil in a cast-iron skillet and warm it over medium-high heat. Sprinkle salt, pepper, the paprika, cumin, and ground fennel on the chicken thighs. When the oil starts to shimmer, place the thighs in the pan, skin side down, and cook until well browned, about 4 minutes. Turn the thighs over and place the pan in the oven. Roast until their internal temperature is 165°F, about 16 minutes. Halfway through, add the tomatoes, garlic, and shallot to the pan.

3   When chicken is fully cooked, remove the pan from the oven and transfer it to a plate. Leave the vegetables in the pan, add the white wine, and place over high heat. Cook for 1 minute, while shaking the pan. Transfer the contents of the pan to the blender, puree until smooth, and season to taste. Set the puree aside.

4   To serve, place some of the tabbouleh on each plate. Top with a chicken thigh and spoon some of the puree over it.

YIELD: 6 SERVINGS

ACTIVE TIME: 30 MINUTES

TOTAL TIME: 2 DAYS

PORCHETTA

5- to 6-lb. skin-on pork belly

1 tablespoon finely chopped fresh rosemary

1 tablespoon finely chopped fresh thyme

1 tablespoon finely chopped fresh sage

2 teaspoons garlic powder

Salt, to taste

1-lb. center-cut pork tenderloin

1   Place the pork belly skin side down on a cutting board. Using a sharp knife, score the flesh in a crosshatch pattern, cutting about ¼ inch deep. Flip the pork belly over and poke small holes in the skin. Turn the pork belly back over and rub the fresh herbs, garlic powder, and salt into the scored flesh. Place the pork tenderloin in the center of the pork belly and then roll the pork belly up so that it retains its length. Tie the rolled pork belly securely with kitchen twine every ½ inch.

2   Transfer the pork belly to a rack with a large pan underneath, place it in the fridge, and leave uncovered for 2 days. This allows the skin to dry out a bit. Blot the pork belly occasionally with paper towels to remove excess moisture.

3   Remove the pork belly from the refrigerator and let it stand at room temperature for 1 hour. Preheat the oven to 480°F. When the pork belly is room temperature, place the rack and the pan in the oven and roast for 35 minutes, turning the porchetta occasionally to ensure even cooking.

4   Reduce the oven temperature to 300°F and cook the porchetta until a meat thermometer inserted into the center reaches 145°F, about 1 to 2 hours. The porchetta's skin should be crispy. If it is not as crispy as you'd like, raise the oven's temperature to 500°F and cook until crispy. Remove from the oven and let the porchetta rest for 15 minutes before slicing.

YIELD: 6 SERVINGS

ACTIVE TIME: 45 MINUTES

TOTAL TIME: 3 HOURS

KOREAN CHICKEN THIGHS WITH SWEET POTATO VERMICELLI

FOR THE MARINADE

1 lemongrass stalk, trimmed and bruised

2 garlic cloves

1-inch piece of fresh ginger, peeled and minced

1 scallion, trimmed and chopped

¼ cup brown sugar

2 tablespoons gochujang

1 tablespoon sesame oil

1 tablespoon rice vinegar

2 tablespoons fish sauce

1 tablespoon black pepper

FOR THE CHICKEN & VERMICELLI

6 skin-on, bone-in chicken thighs

10 oz. sweet potato vermicelli

2 tablespoons olive oil

2 tablespoons sesame oil

2 cups chopped napa cabbage

5 oz. shiitake mushrooms, sliced

1 shallot, sliced thin

1 yellow onion, sliced thin

2 garlic cloves, minced

2-inch piece of fresh ginger, peeled and minced

2 scallions, trimmed and chopped, greens reserved for garnish

¼ cup brown sugar

2 tablespoons fish sauce

¼ cup soy sauce

¼ cup rice vinegar

¼ cup sesame seeds

1   To prepare the marinade, place all of the ingredients in a food processor and blitz until smooth.

2   To begin preparations for the chicken and vermicelli, place the chicken thighs in a resealable bag. Pour half of the marinade over the chicken thighs and marinate in the refrigerator for at least 2 hours. Set the rest of the marinade aside and store in the refrigerator.

3   Remove the chicken from the refrigerator and let it come to room temperature. Fill a Dutch oven with water and bring to a boil. Add the vermicelli and cook until it is nearly al dente, about 6 minutes. Drain, rinse with cold water, and set aside.

4   Preheat the oven to 375°F. Remove the chicken from the refrigerator and place the Dutch oven on the stove. Add the olive oil and warm over medium-high heat. Remove the chicken thighs from the marinade and place them in the pot, skin side down. Cook until a crust forms on the skin, about 5 to 7 minutes. Turn the chicken thighs over, add the reserved marinade, place the pot in the oven, and braise for about 15 to 20 minutes, until the centers of the chicken thighs reach 165°F.

5   While the chicken thighs are braising, place the sesame oil, cabbage, mushrooms, shallot, onion, garlic, ginger, and scallion whites in a skillet and cook over medium heat, stirring frequently, until the cabbage is wilted, about 6 minutes.

6   Place the brown sugar, fish sauce, soy sauce, and rice vinegar in a small bowl and stir until combined. Add this sauce and the vermicelli to the Dutch oven, stir until the noodles are coated, and then add the vegetable mixture to the pot. Top with the scallion greens and sesame seeds and return the pot to the oven for 5 minutes to warm through. Remove from the oven and serve immediately.

YIELD: 6 SERVINGS

ACTIVE TIME: 20 MINUTES

TOTAL TIME: I HOUR AND I5 MINUTES

HEIRLOOM TOMATO & SMOKED CHEDDAR SOUP

2 sticks of unsalted butter

1 small red onion, sliced

3 celery stalks, sliced

10 garlic cloves, sliced

1 tablespoon kosher salt, plus more to taste

½ cup all-purpose flour

8 heirloom tomatoes, chopped

3 cups Marinara Sauce (see page 115)

1 tablespoon tomato paste

4 cups Vegetable Stock (see page 22)

1 Parmesan cheese rind (optional)

1 cup heavy cream

1 cup grated smoked cheddar cheese

10 fresh basil leaves, shredded

Black pepper, to taste

1 Place the butter in a large saucepan and melt over medium heat. Add the onion, celery, garlic, and salt and sauté until the onion is translucent, about 3 minutes.

2 Add the flour and cook until it gives off a nutty aroma, stirring constantly to ensure that it does not brown too quickly. Add the tomatoes, sauce, tomato paste, stock, and, if using, the Parmesan rind. Stir to incorporate and let the soup come to a boil. Reduce the heat so that the soup simmers and cook for 30 minutes. Taste to see if the flavor is to your liking. If not, continue to simmer until it is.

3 Stir the cream, cheddar, and basil into the soup. Remove the Parmesan rind, if using, transfer the soup to a blender, and puree until smooth. Season with salt and pepper and ladle into warmed bowls.

YIELD: 4 SERVINGS

ACTIVE TIME: 20 MINUTES

TOTAL TIME: 24 HOURS

CHIMICHURRI STRIP STEAK WITH OREGANO POTATOES AND ONIONS

FOR THE CHIMICHURRI

2 tablespoons finely chopped fresh oregano

¼ cup olive oil

2 cups fresh parsley

1½ cups fresh cilantro leaves

1 small yellow onion, chopped

2 scallions, trimmed

1 jalapeño pepper, stemmed and seeds and ribs removed

¾ teaspoon kosher salt

¾ teaspoon black pepper

¾ teaspoon onion powder

¾ teaspoon garlic powder

1 tablespoon sugar

⅓ cup water

FOR THE STEAK, POTATOES & ONIONS

1½ lbs. N.Y. strip steaks

Salt and pepper, to taste

1 lb. white sweet potatoes, peeled and diced

1 lb. Yukon Gold potatoes, peeled and diced

1 tablespoon olive oil

2 tablespoons beef tallow

1 large white onion, sliced thin

¼ cup red wine vinegar

⅓ cup dry red wine

1 tablespoon finely chopped fresh oregano

---

1 To prepare the chimichurri sauce, place all of the ingredients in a food processor and blitz until smooth. Transfer half of the sauce and the steaks to an airtight container and let them marinate in the refrigerator overnight. Refrigerate the other half of the sauce in a separate container.

2 Preheat the oven to 375°F. Remove the steaks from the marinade and season both sides with salt. Let the steaks come to room temperature as you cook the potatoes.

3 Place the sweet potatoes, the potatoes, and salt in a large cast-iron skillet. Cover with water, bring to a boil, and cook until the potatoes are tender, about 20 minutes. Drain and set aside.

4. Wipe out the pan, add the olive oil and beef tallow, and warm over medium-high heat. When the oil starts to shimmer, add the steaks and cook until browned on each side, about 4 minutes. Remove the steaks from the pan and set them aside.

5. Place the sweet potatoes, potatoes, onion, and 3 tablespoons of the reserved chimichurri sauce in the pan and cook, stirring continuously, over medium heat until the onion is soft, about 10 minutes. Add the vinegar, wine, and oregano and cook until the vinegar and wine have nearly evaporated, about 5 minutes.

6. Return the steaks to the pan and then place it in the oven. Bake until the steaks are

medium-rare, about 5 minutes. Remove the pan from the oven and serve immediately, topping each portion with some of the remaining chimichurri sauce.

TIP: Beef tallow is the rendered fat of beef, and a great substitute for butter. If you are feeling adventurous and want the authentic taste for this dish, you can ask your local butcher where to purchase it. You can also ask him for some beef fat, grind it in a food processor until fine, and cook it in a slow cooker on low for 6 to 8 hours. Then strain the fat through a coffee filter and store the liquid in the refrigerator until ready to use. To get I cup of tallow you'll need I pound of beef fat.

FOR THE KEFTA

1½ lbs. ground lamb

½ lb. ground beef

½ cup white onion, minced

2 garlic cloves, roasted and mashed

Zest of 1 lemon

1 cup fresh parsley, finely chopped

2 tablespoons finely chopped fresh mint

1 teaspoon cinnamon

2 tablespoons cumin

1 tablespoon paprika

1 teaspoon coriander

Salt and pepper, to taste

¼ cup olive oil

FOR THE SALAD

1 (14 oz.) can of chickpeas, drained and rinsed

½ onion, chopped

½ cup finely chopped fresh cilantro stems

2 tablespoons olive oil

Juice of 1 lemon

¼ teaspoon saffron

1 tablespoon cumin

1 teaspoon cinnamon

½ teaspoon red pepper flakes

Salt and pepper, to taste

YIELD: 4 SERVINGS

ACTIVE TIME: 45 MINUTES

TOTAL TIME: 45 MINUTES

KEFTA WITH CHICKPEA SALAD

1   To begin preparations for the kefta, place all of the ingredients, except for the olive oil, in a mixing bowl and stir until well combined. Place a small bit of the mixture in a skillet and cook over medium heat until it is cooked through. Taste and adjust the seasoning in the mixture as necessary. Form the mixture into 18 ovals and run skewers through them, placing three meatballs on each skewer.

2   Place the olive oil in a Dutch oven and warm over medium-high heat. Working in batches, add three skewers to the pot and sear the

kefta until browned all over, about 8 minutes per batch. Remove the kefta from the pot and set them aside.

3   Return the skewers to the pot, cover it, and remove it from heat. Let stand for 10 minutes so the kefta get cooked through.

4   To prepare the salad, place all of the ingredients in a small mixing bowl and stir until combined. Place the salad on serving plates, top each portion with the kefta, and serve.

YIELD: 6 SERVINGS

ACTIVE TIME: 25 MINUTES

TOTAL TIME: 1 HOUR AND 15 MINUTES

JAMBALAYA

½ lb. andouille sausage, sliced

½ lb. small shrimp, peeled and deveined

¼ cup olive oil

4 boneless, skinless chicken thighs, chopped

2 yellow onions, chopped

1 large green bell pepper, stemmed, seeds and ribs removed, and chopped

2 celery stalks, chopped

3 garlic cloves, minced

3 plum tomatoes, chopped

2 bay leaves

2 tablespoons paprika

2 tablespoons dried thyme

1 tablespoon garlic powder

1 tablespoon onion powder

1 teaspoon cayenne pepper

1½ cups long-grain white rice

2 tablespoons Worcestershire sauce

Hot sauce, to taste

3 cups Chicken Stock (see page 37)

Salt and pepper, to taste

Scallions, trimmed and chopped, for garnish

1   Place the sausage in a Dutch oven and cook over medium-high heat until browned, about 8 minutes. Remove the sausage and set it aside. Add the shrimp and cook for 1 minute on each side. Remove the shrimp and set it aside.

2   Add the oil, chicken, onions, bell pepper, and celery to the Dutch oven. Cook until the vegetables start to caramelize and the chicken is browned and cooked through, 6 to 8 minutes. Add the garlic and cook until fragrant, about 2 minutes.

3   Add the tomatoes, the bay leaves, and all of the seasonings. Simmer for 30 minutes, stirring occasionally.

4   Stir in the rice, Worcestershire sauce, hot sauce, and stock. Return the sausage to the pot, reduce heat to medium-low, cover, and cook for 25 minutes.

5   Return the shrimp to the pan, cover, and cook for 5 minutes. Season with salt and pepper, ladle the stew into bowls, and garnish with the scallions.

YIELD: 6 SERVINGS

ACTIVE TIME: 40 MINUTES

TOTAL TIME: 2 HOURS AND 15 MINUTES

PAELLA

½ cup fresh parsley, chopped

2 tablespoons olive oil

1 lemon, ½ juiced, ½ cut into wedges

Salt and pepper, to taste

6 boneless, skinless chicken thighs

24 shrimp, peeled and deveined

½ lb. Spanish chorizo, sliced

¼ cup diced pancetta

½ large white onion, chopped

1 bell pepper, stemmed, seeds and ribs removed, and minced

4 garlic cloves, minced

1 cup chopped plum tomatoes

3 cups short-grain rice

6 cups Chicken Stock (see page 37)

1 teaspoon saffron

1 tablespoon pimenton (Spanish paprika)

24 PEI mussels, rinsed well and debearded

1 cup peas

1   Preheat the oven to 450°F. Place 2 tablespoons of the parsley, the olive oil, lemon juice, salt, and pepper in a bowl and stir to combine. Add the chicken thighs to the bowl and marinate for 30 minutes to 1 hour.

2   Warm a cast-iron skillet over medium-high heat. Add the chicken to the pan and sear on each side for 3 to 5 minutes. Remove the chicken from the pan and set it aside.

3   Place the shrimp in the pan and cook for 1 minute on each side, until the shrimp is cooked approximately three-quarters of the way through. Remove the shrimp from the pan and set it aside.

4   Place the chorizo, pancetta, onion, bell pepper, and half of the garlic in the skillet and cook until the onion starts to caramelize, about 10 minutes. Season with salt and pepper and add the tomatoes, rice, stock, the remaining garlic and parsley, saffron, and pimenton. Cook for 10 minutes, stirring often.

5   Reduce heat to medium-low and press the chicken into the mixture in the skillet. Cover the skillet and cook for 10 minutes.

6   Uncover the skillet and add the mussels, shrimp, and peas. Cover the skillet, place it in the oven, and cook until the majority of the mussels have opened and the rice is tender, about 12 minutes. Discard any mussels that do not open. If the rice is still a bit crunchy, remove the mussels and shrimp, set them aside, return pan to the oven, and cook until the rice is tender. Serve with the lemon wedges.

YIELD: 4 SERVINGS

ACTIVE TIME: 45 MINUTES

TOTAL TIME: 5 HOURS AND 30 MINUTES

LAMB KEBABS WITH SUCCOTASH

FOR THE LAMB KEBABS

2 lbs. boneless leg of lamb, cut into 1½-inch cubes

Salt and pepper, to taste

3 tablespoons olive oil

1½ cups red wine

4 garlic cloves, crushed

1 shallot, minced

2 teaspoons finely chopped fresh rosemary

1 teaspoon cumin

2 red onions, chopped

2 red bell peppers, stemmed, seeds and ribs removed, and chopped

FOR THE SUCCOTASH

1 cup sliced mushroom caps

1 red onion, minced

4 cups corn kernels

1 red bell pepper, stemmed, seeds and ribs removed, and chopped

2 cups fresh or frozen edamame

1 tablespoon unsalted butter

Salt and pepper, to taste

1 tablespoon finely chopped fresh marjoram

½ cup fresh basil leaves, chopped

1   To begin preparations for the lamb kebabs, place all of the ingredients, except for the red onions and peppers, in a large resealable plastic bag. Toss to combine, place the bag in the refrigerator, and marinate for 4 hours. If time allows, marinate the lamb overnight.

2   Remove the lamb from the refrigerator about 30 minutes before you are going to start grilling. Transfer the lamb to a platter and let it rest at room temperature. If using bamboo skewers, soak them in water. Preheat your gas or charcoal grill to medium-high heat (about 450°F).

3   To prepare the succotash, place a large cast-iron skillet over medium heat, add the mushrooms and cook until they release their liquid and start to brown, about 8 minutes. Reduce heat to low and cook until the mushrooms are a deep brown, about 15 minutes. Place the onion in the skillet, raise heat to medium-high, and sauté until it starts to soften, about 5 minutes. Add the corn, bell pepper, and edamame and sauté until the edamame is tender, about 6 minutes. Add the butter and stir until it has melted and coated all of the vegetables. Season with salt and pepper, stir in the marjoram and basil, remove the pan from heat, and set it aside.

4   Place approximately 4 pieces of lamb on each skewer, making sure to arrange the pieces of onion and pepper in between each piece of lamb.

5   Place the skewers on the grill and cook, while turning, until the lamb is medium-rare and browned all over, about 10 minutes. Transfer the kebabs to a large cutting board and let them rest for 5 minutes before serving with the succotash.

FOR THE DUMPLINGS

2 lbs. zucchini, trimmed and grated

1 tablespoon kosher salt

1 small red onion, chopped

¼ cup raw cashews

2 garlic cloves, minced

1-inch piece of fresh ginger, peeled and minced

4 bird's eye chili peppers, stemmed, seeds and ribs removed, and minced

½ cup chickpea flour

2 tablespoons finely chopped fresh cilantro

4 cups vegetable oil

FOR THE SAUCE

2 tablespoons olive oil

1 teaspoon cumin seeds

1 red onion, chopped

4 bird's eye chili peppers, stemmed, seeds and ribs removed, and minced

2 tablespoons raw cashews

2 tablespoons golden raisins

1 (28 oz.) can of diced tomatoes, drained

1 teaspoon kosher salt

¼ cup milk

¼ cup heavy cream

¼ teaspoon turmeric

2 pinches of black pepper

2 pinches of cinnamon

2 pinches of ground cloves

2 pinches of grated fresh nutmeg

2 pinches of cardamom

YIELD: 6 SERVINGS

ACTIVE TIME: 30 MINUTES

TOTAL TIME: I HOUR AND 30 MINUTES

DUDHI KOFTA CURRY

I To begin preparations for the dumplings, place the grated zucchini in a colander, add the salt, and stir to combine. Let the zucchini sit for 20 minutes.

2 While the zucchini is sitting, begin preparations for the sauce. Place the olive oil in a saucepan and warm it over medium-high heat. When the oil starts to shimmer, add the cumin seeds, cook for about 1 minute, until they are fragrant, and then add the onion, chilies, cashews, and raisins. Sauté until the onion and cashews are slightly browned, about 5 minutes. Add the tomatoes and salt, cook for another 2 minutes, transfer the mixture to a food processor, and puree until smooth. Set the puree aside and resume preparations for the dumplings.

3 Place the onion, cashews, garlic, ginger, and chilies in a food processor and blitz until the mixture becomes a chunky paste.

4 Place the zucchini in a kitchen towel and wring it to remove as much liquid as possible. Place the zucchini in a mixing bowl and add the onion-and-cashew paste. Stir to combine, add the chickpea flour and cilantro, and fold to incorporate. The dough should be just slightly wet.

5 Place the vegetable oil in a Dutch oven and heat it to 300°F. As the oil warms, form tablespoons of the dough into balls and place them on a parchment-lined baking sheet. When the oil is ready, place the dumplings in the oil and fry until golden brown, about 5 minutes. Work in batches if necessary. Transfer the cooked dumplings to a paper towel–lined plate to drain and resume preparations for the sauce.

6 Return the puree to the saucepan, add the remaining ingredients, and stir to combine. Heat until warmed through, ladle into warmed bowls, and divide the dumplings between them.

YIELD: 6 SERVINGS

ACTIVE TIME: 1 HOUR

TOTAL TIME: 24 HOURS

STEAMED PORK BUNS

FOR THE PORK BELLY

6 cups water

1 teaspoon fennel seeds

2 star anise pods

1 cinnamon stick

1 teaspoon peppercorns

6 whole cloves

1 bay leaf

¼ cup kosher salt

1½ lbs. pork belly, fat side scored ¼ inch deep

Pickled Tomatoes (see sidebar), for serving

FOR THE BUNS

1 teaspoon active dry yeast

3 tablespoons water, at room temperature

1 cup bread flour, plus more as needed

4 teaspoons sugar

2 teaspoons nonfat milk powder

1 teaspoon kosher salt

⅛ teaspoon baking powder

⅛ teaspoon baking soda

4 teaspoons vegetable shortening, plus more as needed

1   Start the preparations the night before you plan to serve this dish. To prepare the pork belly, place the water, fennel seeds, star anise pods, cinnamon stick, peppercorns, whole cloves, bay leaf, and salt in a saucepan and bring to a boil. Turn off the heat and let the mixture cool completely. Place the pork belly in a roasting pan and pour the cooled liquid into the pan. Place the pan in the refrigerator overnight.

2   Preheat oven to 450°F and rinse the pork belly. Place the pork belly on a rimmed baking sheet, scored side up, place it in the oven, and roast for 30 minutes. Lower the temperature to 275°F and roast the pork belly until it is tender, but not mushy, about 1 hour. While the pork belly is roasting, prepare the buns.

3 To begin preparations for the buns, place the yeast and water in the mixing bowl of a stand mixer fitted with a dough hook and let sit until the mixture becomes foamy, about 10 minutes. Add the remaining ingredients and mix on low for 10 minutes. Cover the bowl with a kitchen towel and place it in a naturally warm spot until the dough doubles in size, about 45 minutes.

4 Place the risen dough on a flour-dusted work surface and cut it into 12 pieces. Roll them into balls, cover with plastic wrap, and let them rise for 30 minutes.

5 Cut a dozen 4-inch squares of parchment paper. Roll each ball into a 4-inch-long oval. Grease a chopstick with shortening, gently press the chopstick down in the middle of each oval, and fold the dough over to create a bun. Place each bun on a square of parchment and let them rest for another 30 minutes.

6 When the pork belly is done, remove and let it rest for 20 minutes. Place 1 inch of water in a saucepan and bring to a boil. Place a steaming tray in the pan and, working in batches if necessary, place the buns in the steamer tray, making sure to leave them on the squares of parchment. Steam for 10 minutes. Slice the pork belly thin and fill the buns with it. Top with the Pickled Tomatoes and serve.

PICKLED TOMATOES

Place ¼ cup white wine vinegar, 1½ tablespoons brown sugar, 2 teaspoons kosher salt, ½ teaspoon minced garlic, 2 teaspoons mustard seeds, ¼ teaspoon black pepper, 1 teaspoon cumin, ¼ teaspoon cayenne pepper, ¼ teaspoon turmeric, and 1½ tablespoons olive oil in a saucepan and bring to a simmer over medium heat. Remove from heat, let cool completely, and then add 2 chopped tomatoes. Cover and chill in the refrigerator overnight.

1 lb. flank steak, trimmed

1 (12 oz.) bottle of beer

1 tablespoon toasted sesame oil

3 garlic cloves, sliced thin

2-inch piece of fresh ginger, peeled and grated

½ cup soy sauce

¾ cup water

1½ tablespoons molasses

1 teaspoon sriracha, plus more to taste

⅔ cup firmly packed brown sugar

¾ lb. Chinese egg noodles

2 cups peanut oil, plus ¼ cup

2 tablespoons cornstarch

8 baby bok choy, quartered and blanched

Salt, to taste

YIELD: 4 SERVINGS

ACTIVE TIME: 45 MINUTES

TOTAL TIME: 4 HOURS

MONGOLIAN BEEF WITH CRISPY CHOW MEIN

1   Place the flank steak and beer in a large plastic bag. Place the bag in a shallow pan and marinate in the refrigerator for 3 hours, turning the bag over a few times. Let the steak come to room temperature before cooking.

2   Place a small saucepan over medium heat for 1 minute. Add the sesame oil, heat for 1 minute, add the garlic and ginger, and sauté until fragrant, about 1 minute. Add the soy sauce and ½ cup of the water and bring to a boil. Add the molasses, sriracha, and brown sugar and cook, while stirring frequently, until the sauce thickens, about 5 minutes. Remove the pan from heat and set it aside.

3   Bring a large pot of water to a boil and add the noodles. Cook until they are tender but still chewy, 2 to 3 minutes. Drain and place them on a kitchen towel to dry.

4   Working in two batches, heat a medium skillet over low heat for 2 to 3 minutes. Add 2 tablespoons of the peanut oil and raise the heat to medium-high. When the oil starts to shimmer, add half of the noodles and cook, without touching them, for 3 to 4 minutes, until they are golden brown and crispy. Carefully flip the cake of noodles over and cook for 3 minutes. Transfer to a paper towel-lined plate to dry, add 2 more tablespoons of the oil, and repeat with the remaining noodles.

5   Slice the steak into thin strips, cutting against the grain. Place the strips in a medium bowl with the cornstarch and toss until evenly coated. Heat a deep saucepan over low heat for 2 minutes. Add the remaining oil, raise the heat to medium-high, and heat the oil until it reaches 360°F. Add 4 slices of steak, cook for 1½ minutes, remove with a slotted spoon, and transfer to a paper towel-lined platter. Cover with aluminum foil and repeat with the remaining slices of steak.

6   Transfer the cooked steak to a medium bowl, add ¾ cup of the sauce, and toss to coat. Cut the crispy noodle cakes in half and place one piece on each of the serving plates. Top each cake with the steak and bok choy, season with salt, and serve with the remaining sauce.

YIELD: 8 SERVINGS   **ACTIVE TIME:** 1 HOUR   **TOTAL TIME:** 1 HOUR AND 30 MINUTES

BUTTERNUT SQUASH & SAGE CANNELLONI

FOR THE FILLING

2 lbs. butternut squash, halved and seeded

5 tablespoons olive oil

5 garlic cloves, minced

1½ cups whole-milk ricotta cheese

1 cup grated Parmesan cheese

12 fresh sage leaves, sliced thin

1 teaspoon grated fresh nutmeg

Salt and white pepper, to taste

FOR THE CANNELLONI

Dough from Tagliatelle (see page 235)

Semolina flour, as needed

Salt, to taste

½ tablespoon olive oil, plus more as needed

1 To begin preparations for the filling, preheat the oven to 375°F. Brush the flesh of the squash with 1 tablespoon of the olive oil and place the squash on a parchment-lined baking sheet, cut side down. Place the baking sheet in the oven and roast until the squash is fork-tender, 40 to 45 minutes. Remove the squash from the oven and let it cool. When it is cool enough to handle, scoop the flesh into a wide, shallow bowl and mash it until smooth.

2 Warm a large skillet over low heat for 2 to 3 minutes. Add 2 tablespoons of the oil and the garlic and raise the heat to medium. Sauté for 1 minute, remove the pan from heat, and transfer the garlic and oil to the bowl with the pureed squash. Add the cheeses, half of the sage, the nutmeg, salt, and pepper and stir to combine.

3 To begin preparations for the cannelloni, roll the dough through a pasta maker until the sheets are about 1⁄16 inch thick. Lay the sheets on lightly floured, parchment paper–lined baking sheets. Working with one sheet at a time, place it on a lightly floured work surface in front of you. Using a pastry cutter, cut each sheet into as many 4½- to 5-inch squares as possible. Place the finished squares on another lightly floured, parchment-lined baking sheet so they don't touch. As you run out of room, lightly dust them with flour,

cover with another sheet of parchment, and arrange more squares on top of that. Repeat with all the pasta sheets. Gather any scraps together into a ball, put it through the pasta machine to create additional pasta sheets, and cut those as well.

4   Bring a large pot of water to a boil. Once it's boiling, add salt and stir to dissolve. Add the squares and carefully stir for the first minute to prevent any sticking. Cook until they are just tender, about 2 minutes. Drain, rinse under cold water, and toss with a teaspoon of olive oil to keep them from sticking together.

5   Generously coat a baking dish large enough to fit all the filled cannelloni in a single layer with olive oil. To fill the cannelloni, place a pasta square in front of you. Place ¼ cup of the squash mixture in the center of the square and shape it into a rough cylinder. Roll the pasta square around the filling into a tube and transfer to the prepared baking dish, seam side down. Repeat with remaining sheets and filling. When the baking dish is filled, brush the tops of the cannelloni with the remaining olive oil.

6   Preheat the oven to 375°F and place a rack in the middle position. Put the baking dish in the oven and bake until the cannelloni are very hot and begin to turn golden brown, about 20 minutes. Top with the remaining sage and serve.

METRIC CONVERSIONS

U.S. Measurement	Approximate Metric Liquid Measurement	Approximate Metric Dry Measurement
1 teaspoon	5 ml	5 g
1 tablespoon or ½ ounce	15 ml	14 g
1 ounce or ⅛ cup	30 ml	29 g
¼ cup or 2 ounces	60 ml	57 g
⅓ cup	80 ml	76 g
½ cup or 4 ounces	120 ml	113 g
⅔ cup	160 ml	151 g
¾ cup or 6 ounces	180 ml	170 g
1 cup or 8 ounces or ½ pint	240 ml	227 g
1½ cups or 12 ounces	350 ml	340 g
2 cups or 1 pint or 16 ounces	475 ml	454 g
3 cups or 1½ pints	700 ml	680 g
4 cups or 2 pints or 1 quart	950 ml	908 g

INDEX

ABOUT CIDER MILL PRESS BOOK PUBLISHERS

Good ideas ripen with time. From seed to harvest, Cider Mill Press brings fine reading, information, and entertainment together between the covers of its creatively crafted books. Our Cider Mill bears fruit twice a year, publishing a new crop of titles each spring and fall.

CIDER MILL PRESS

BOOK PUBLISHERS

"Where Good Books Are Ready for Press"

VISIT US ON THE WEB AT
cidermillpress.com

OR WRITE TO US AT
PO Box 454
12 Spring St.
Kennebunkport, Maine 04046